TEMPO

Olivia Johnston

Chris Barker and Libby Mitchell

WORKBOOK 2

MACMILLAN

G000320734

Module	Unit		
Module 1	1 You mustn't do that!	Grammar file	page 4
		Vocabulary	page 6
		Dialogue work	page 7
		Grammar practice: Present simple; *must / mustn't* for obligation and prohibition; *like* + verb + *ing*; *be like* descriptions	page 7
		Skills development	page 10
		Study tips	page 11
		Talk time	page 12
		Let's check	page 13
	2 Mum doesn't let me do anything	Grammar file	page 14
		Vocabulary	page 16
		Dialogue work	page 16
		Grammar practice: verb *let*; *would like*; *How much is/are ...?*; *How much* + noun ...?; *How many* + noun ...?	page 17
		Culture spot: Pocket money	page 20
		Portfolio	page 21
		Let's read	page 22
		Let's check	page 23
		Extra!	page 24
Module 2	3 What are we doing at the weekend?	Grammar file	page 26
		Vocabulary	page 28
		Dialogue work	page 28
		Grammar practice: Present continuous revision and for future use; Future with *going to*; *Let's ...*; *Why don't we ...?*	page 29
		Skills development	page 32
		Study tips	page 33
		Talk time	page 34
		Let's check	page 35
	4 I'll carry the picnic basket	Grammar file	page 36
		Vocabulary	page 38
		Dialogue work	page 38
		Grammar practice: Future with *will* for offers, predictions and decisions; *should*; possessive pronouns	page 39
		Culture spot: Edinburgh	page 42
		Portfolio	page 43
		Let's read	page 44
		Let's check	page 45
		Extra!	page 46
Module 3	5 The highest mountain	Grammar file	page 48
		Vocabulary	page 50
		Dialogue work	page 50
		Grammar practice: comparatives and superlatives of adjectives; *too* + adjective; *not* + adjective *enough*	page 51
		Skills development	page 54
		Study tips	page 55
		Talk time	page 56
		Let's check	page 57
	6 Where were you last night?	Grammar file	page 58
		Vocabulary	page 60
		Dialogue work	page 60
		Grammar practice: Past simple *be*; Past simple of regular verbs; past time adverbials *last Saturday,* etc.	page 61
		Culture spot: A weekend in Dorset	page 64
		Portfolio	page 65
		Let's read	page 66
		Let's check	page 67
		Extra!	page 68

Module	Unit		
Module 4	7 We made lots of pancakes!	Grammar file	page 70
		Vocabulary	page 72
		Dialogue work	page 72
		Grammar practice: quantifiers *a few / a little / lots of / plenty of / many / much*	page 73
		Skills development	page 76
		Study tips	page 77
		Talk time	page 78
		Let's check	page 79
	8 That was 500 years ago!	Grammar file	page 80
		Vocabulary	page 82
		Dialogue work	page 83
		Grammar practice: Past simple regular and irregular verbs; *ago*; *could* for requests; giving directions; imperatives	page 83
		Culture spot: The Tower of London	page 86
		Portfolio	page 87
		Let's read	page 88
		Let's check	page 89
		Extra!	page 90
Module 5	9 Were you chatting up the boys?	Grammar file	page 92
		Vocabulary	page 94
		Dialogue work	page 94
		Grammar practice: Past continuous; reflexive pronouns	page 95
		Skills development	page 98
		Study tips	page 99
		Talk time	page 100
		Let's check	page 101
	10 Would you like to meet Liberty X?	Grammar file	page 102
		Vocabulary	page 104
		Dialogue work	page 104
		Grammar practice: *Would like to* + verb; regular and irregular adverbs; Present simple and Present continuous; Past simple and Past continuous	page 105
		Culture spot: Holiday in the USA	page 108
		Portfolio	page 109
		Let's read	page 110
		Let's check	page 111
		Extra!	page 112
	Portfolio Dossier	Write a letter describing a trip	page 114
		Vocabulary builder	page 116

GRAMMAR FILE

must/mustn't

Affirmative

I must go.
You must go.
She/He/It must go.
We must go.
You must go.
They must go.

- We use *must* to say that something is necessary, e.g.
  You must go to bed now. It's very late.
  We must get up early tomorrow.
  Our train is at six in the morning.

Negative

Long form

I must not be late.
You must not be late.
She/He/It must not be late.
We must not be late.
You must not be late.
They must not be late.

Short form

I mustn't be late.
You mustn't be late.
She/He/It mustn't be late.
We mustn't be late.
You mustn't be late.
They mustn't be late.

- We use *must not* or *mustn't* to say that something is forbidden or the wrong thing to do, e.g. *You mustn't swim in that lake. It's very dangerous. We mustn't make a noise. My little brother is in bed.*

Questions

Must I go?
Must you go?
Must she/he/it go?
Must we go?
Must you go?
Must they go?

- *must* is followed by the base form of the verb – the infinitive without *to*, e.g. *You must bring a packed lunch to school tomorrow.* NOT: ~~You must to bring a packed lunch to school tomorrow.~~

Short answers

Affirmative

Yes, I must.
Yes, you must.
Yes, she/he/it must.
Yes, we must.
Yes, you must.
Yes, they must.

Negative

No, I mustn't.
No, you mustn't.
No she/he/it mustn't.
No, we mustn't.
No, you mustn't.
No, they mustn't.

- There is only one form of the verb for all persons, singular and plural.

wh- questions

When must I be there?
Where must you go?
What must he/she do?
Why must we stop?
How must we do it?
Who must you see?
How long must they stay?

- We change the order of the subject and verb in questions, e.g. *Must I do all the exercises on this page? What time must we meet?*

The present simple tense – revision

Affirmative

I/You/We/They start at nine o'clock.
He/She/It starts at nine o'clock.

Negative

I/You/We/They don't start at eight o'clock.
He/She/It doesn't start at eight o'clock.

Questions

Do I/you/we/they finish at four?
Does he/she/it finish at four?

Short answers

Affirmative	Negative
Yes, I/you/we/they do.	No, I/you/we/they don't.
Yes, he/she/it does.	No, he/she/it doesn't.

Wh- questions

What time do I start?
When do you finish?
Where does she live?
Why do we study History?
How do they get to school?

- We use the Present simple tense to talk about likes and dislikes. We also use it to talk about permanent situations, things that don't change and routines.

- In the Present simple, the verb is the same for all persons except the third person singular.

- In the affirmative form, the third person singular always ends in s, e.g. *He lives in my street. She goes to my school.*

- Don't forget: we add *es* to the base form of verbs ending in *o, ss, ch, sh* e.g. *go/goes, kiss/kisses, watch/watches, push/pushes.* With verbs ending in *y*, we change the *y* to *ies*, e.g. *cry/cries, try/tries.* BUT: *play/plays, buy/buys, say/says.*

like + gerund (*-ing* form)

I like getting letters.
She likes playing tennis.
You don't like writing letters.
He doesn't like getting up early.
Does she like cooking?
Do they like singing?
What does she like doing in her free time?
Where do they like going on holiday?

- The verb *like* is often followed by the gerund (*-ing* form, e.g. *I like swimming. Do you like sitting in the sun? They don't like talking on the phone*).

- There are spelling rules for forming the gerund:

  – With verbs ending in one *e*, we drop the *e* and add *-ing*, e.g. *ride – riding, write – writing.*

  – With one-syllable verbs that end in one vowel and one consonant (NOT *w* or *y*), we double the last consonant and add *-ing*, e.g. *run – running, sit – sitting, swim – swimming, get – getting.*

be like for descriptions

What's Andy like? He's nice but he's a bit quiet.
What are your grandparents like?
They're really funny. They talk all the time!
What's the weather like in Ireland? It rains a lot.
What's your room like? It's blue and white and it's got a view of the sea.

- We ask the question *What is/are …like?* when we want a description. We can use it about things, animals or people, e.g. *What's your new house like? What are your teachers like?*

- We do not use the word *like* in our answer, e.g. *What's your new house like? It's got a big garden and I can see the sea from my room.*

You mustn't do that!

Vocabulary

1 Use the words in the box and the clues below to complete the crossword.

annoying	funny	helpful	loyal	patient	sporty
clever	generous	kind	naughty	shy	strict

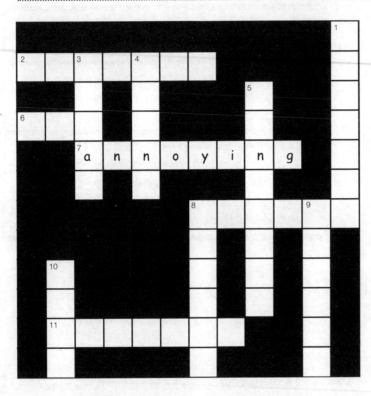

Across

2 He likes helping people. He's very ... .

6 She's frightened of new people and she's very quiet. She's ... .

7 My little brother is very ... . He often takes my CDs and clothes and I can't find them.

8 She can't go to the cinema with her friends. Her parents are very ... .

11 My cat sometimes jumps on the table and eats my food. She's ... .

Down

1 You can't have dinner now. It isn't ready. You must be ... for an hour.

3 His favourite football team is Manchester United. He always goes to their matches. He is a ... fan.

4 'Do you like The Simpsons?' 'Yes, it makes me laugh. I think it's a very ... programme.'

5 'Do your grandparents give you big birthday presents?' 'Yes, they do. They're very ... .'

8 He's in the football team, the swimming team and the tennis team. He is very ... .

9 She can speak four languages and she's very good at Maths and Science. She's very ... .

10 My big sister always helps me with my homework. She is very ... .

2 Read the description and write each girl's name in the correct space.

- Amy is tall with short fair hair. She doesn't wear glasses.
- Beth is of medium height with long dark hair.
- Maria is short with medium length dark hair.
- Jade is tall and wears glasses.

Dialogue work

3 **Use the words to complete the dialogue.**

annoying	do	listens	takes
~~brother~~	does	mustn't	you
computer	listen	plays	

Alex What's your little ......**brother**.. like?

Kate He's really (**1**)...................................... .

Alex Why?

Kate He always (**2**).................... my things.

Alex What things?

Kate CDs, clothes, (**3**).. games.

Alex What (**4**).................... he do with them?

Kate He (**5**).................... to the CDs, wears my T-shirts and (**6**).................... the computer games.

Alex What (**7**).................... you say to him?

Kate I say to him, 'You (**8**).................... take my things, you annoying little boy.'

Alex Does he (**9**).................... to you?

Kate Are (**10**).................... joking? Of course he doesn't.

Grammar practice

4 **Choose the correct form of the verb.**

I (must / mustn't) get my glasses. I can't see the video.

1 You (must / mustn't) eat sweets in class.

2 I (must / mustn't) go to bed early tonight. I'm very tired.

3 You (must / mustn't) listen to this CD. It's brilliant.

4 Lala, you bad cat, you (must / mustn't) drink my milk.

5 We (must / mustn't) forget to give our homework to Miss Ranieri.

6 Tom, you (must / mustn't) come in now. It's time for bed.

7 I (must / mustn't) tidy my room. I can't find anything.

8 Ssh! We (must / mustn't) talk in the library.

9 You (must / mustn't) eat the chocolate cake. It's for the party tomorrow.

10 You (must / mustn't) send granny a card. It's her birthday soon.

5 **Use the prompts to write pairs of sentences in the Present simple.**

Kate / live (✔) / in London. [She / live (✗) in Moreton.]
Kate lives in London. She doesn't live in Moreton.

1 Sophie / play (✔) / tennis. [She / play (✗) / football.]

....

....

2 You / come (✔) / to school by bus. [You / come (✗) / by car.]

....

....

3 My cat / like (✔) / pop music. [She / like (✗) / rap.]

....

....

4 I / study (✔) French. [I / study (✗) / German.]

....

6 **Use the prompts to write questions in the Present simple. Then match the questions to the answers.**

(Alex / like) pasta?
Does Alex like pasta? .... [a]

1 What (you / have) for breakfast?

....

.... [ ]

2 Which school (your sister / go) to?

....

.... [ ]

3 What time (your parents / start) work?

....

.... [ ]

4 (your cat / sleep) on your bed?

....

.... [ ]

5 (Rose and Lila / wear) glasses?

....

.... [ ]

a) ~~He loves it.~~   **d)** Fruit juice and cereal.
b) Hurlingham Girls' School   **e)** Yes, every night!
c) No, they don't.   **f)** Nine o'clock, usually.

7 **Complete the conversation. Write the verbs in the correct form of the Present simple.**

Jack (your brother / go) ...Does your brother go.. to Fitness First Sports Club?

Adam (No, he / not). ....No, he doesn't...........

Jack Which sports club (he / go) (**1**) .... to?

Adam It's called Sports Plus.

Jack What sports (he / do) (**2**) .... there?

Adam Football, basketball and swimming.

Jack (he / play) (**3**) .... tennis at his club?

Adam (No, he / not) (**4**) .... (He / not like) (**5**) .... tennis. Why (you / want) (**6**) .... to know?

Jack (I / want) (**7**) .... to find a new tennis partner. (I / not like) (**8**) .... playing tennis with Liam. (He / always get) (**9**).................................... angry with me!

Adam (you / know) (**10**) .... Joey Delaney?

Jack (Yes, I). (**11**) ....

Adam He likes playing tennis. (you / want) (**12**) .... his telephone number?

Jack Yes, please.

8 **Complete the questions in the Present simple using the correct words from the box. Then answer the questions.**

| get up | ~~go~~ | have | play | ride | sing | swim | watch | wear |

you / like .... to bed late?

Do you like going to bed late?

Yes, I do. / No, I don't.

1 you / like .... breakfast in bed?

....

....

2 you / like .... socks in bed?

....

....

3 you / like .... computer games?

....

....

4 you / like .... early?

....

....

5 you / like .... in cold water?

....

....

6 you / like .... in the shower?

....

....

7 you / like .... sport on TV?

....

....

8 you / like .... your bike in the park?

....

....

9 Complete the dialogue with the correct form of the verbs.

Lara Our cat Kiki is black and white.

Josh <u>Does she like eating</u> (she / like / eat)?

Lara Yes, she ....<u>does</u>..... (✔). She really ....<u>likes</u>..... (like) her food.

Josh What (**1**) .... (she / eat)?

Lara She (**2**) .... (have) cat food. And we sometimes (**3**) .... (give) her milk. She (**4**) .... (sit) on the table at breakfast time.

Josh What (**5**) .... (your Mum / say)?

Lara She (**6**) .... (not / like) it. She (**7**) .... (get) angry with Kiki.

Josh What else (**8**) .... (Kiki / like / do)?

Lara She (**9**) .... (like / sleep)!

Josh (**10**) .... (she sleep) on your bed?

Lara No, she (**11**) .... (✗) . She (**12**) .... (like) my sister's bed. It's nice and big!

Josh (**13**) .... (she / like / play)?

Lara Yes, she (**14**) .... (✔). She (**15**) .... (like / run) down the corridor with a little ball.

Josh (**16**) .... (she / like / listen) to music?

Lara She (**17**) .... (not / like) music. But she (**18**) .... (like/ watch) animal programmes on TV.

10 Write questions with *What's ... like?* Write answers using the words in the box and the pictures.

naughty	funny	generous	clever
helpful	~~strict~~	sporty	

Q: What's Mrs Clayton like?
A: She's very strict.

1 Q: .... Serena ....?
  A: .... very ....

2 Q: .... Woofer ....?
  A: .... quite ....

3 Q: .... Mr Stevens ....?
  A: .... very ....

4 Q: .... your sister ....?
  A: .... quite ....

5 Q: .... your aunt ....?
  A: .... very ....

6 Q: .... your brother, Tim ....?
  A: .... quite ....

Read

My Family
by Josie Chadwick
Year 7

There are five people in my family. My mother's name is Frances but everyone calls her Fran **for short**. She's tall with red hair. She's a teacher. [.d.]. She's quite strict at home. For example, I can't stay up late on weekdays. 1 [....]. But I can invite friends to **sleep over.**

My father is called Alan. He works in a big **computer company**. 2 [....]. Sometimes he cooks and plays football with my brother at the same time! My Mum **gets mad** with him because of the mess in the kitchen. He's quite funny my dad. He and I laugh a lot together. And his **fried chicken** and chips is delicious!

I'm twelve and my name is Josie. I go to Chiswick Secondary School. I'm quite tall and I've got long hair. 3 [....]. I also like music, computer games and **chatting** to my friends on the phone.

My brother, Jack, is eight years old and he goes to Hillgate Primary School. 4 [....]. He often takes my CDs from my room. 5 [....]. He also likes reading my **comics** in his room.

My grandmother lives with us too. Her name is Caroline. She's sixty-two. She likes making **clothes**. She makes me skirts and dresses. She's very kind. 6 [....]. And she buys videos and books for my brother.

Oh there's another person in my family. 7 [....]. It's a cat. Her name's Lily. She's my cat and she loves me. She's very loyal. She **follows** me everywhere. 8 [....]. She's got blue eyes and a very **loud meow**. I know because she wakes me up with it every morning!

1 **Read Josie's essay. Where should these sentences go?**

a) And she always sleeps on my bed.
b) And then I can't find them.
c) And at weekends, I can't stay out after nine o'clock.
d) ~~But she doesn't work at my school.~~
e) Well, it isn't a person.
f) He likes cooking and football.
g) He's a very annoying boy.
h) I'm quite sporty.
i) She often helps me to tidy my room.

2 **Read the text again and translate these words. If you don't know them, guess and check in a dictionary or with your teacher.**

for short ....

sleep over ....

computer company ....

gets mad ....

fried chicken ....

chatting ....

comics ....

clothes ....

follows ....

loud meow ....

Study tips

3 **Writing in English is easier if you use the words and structures you know. You can be interesting even with simple language by giving examples like this:**

Statement	Example
My grandfather is funny.	He often wears a big red hat and rides his bicycle in our garden.
My sister is annoying.	She's very clever but she never helps me with my homework.
My dog, Rufus, is a bit shy.	He sometimes hides under the bed.

Write

4 **Write about your family. Write a paragraph about each person. Start like this:**

There are .... (*how many?*) people

in my family. My ....'s name is

.... (He/She) is (tall/short/of

medium height) with .... hair and

.... eyes. (He/She) is (quite/very)

.... (*write a personality adjective*).

For example, ...

.... (He/She) likes ....

.... and .... ing.

....

....

....

....

....

....

....

....

....

....

....

....

....

....

....

....

....

Talk time

1 **Write the phrases in the correct balloons.**

- It's not fair!
- It's only a toy.
- It's time for a walk.
- Sorry!
- Stop it!

12

Let's check

1 **Complete each sentence with the correct word.**

> ~~kind~~   shy   funny
> naughty   clever

'I can drive you to the station.' 'Oh thank you. That's very ..kind....'

1 I laugh a lot with Andy. He's very ....

2 She's good at all her school subjects. She's very

....

3 He's .... at school. He draws on the desks and eats chewing gum in class.

4 My little brother is frightened of visitors. He's a bit

....

2 **Choose the correct word to describe each speaker.**

> loyal   ~~annoying~~   generous
> sporty   helpful

'I'm right and you're wrong. I'm right, stupid. I'm right, stupid. I'm right, stupid.' ....annoying.....

1 'Let's play football or tennis this morning. Then let's go swimming in the afternoon.' ....

2 'Here's £50 for your birthday. And I want to take you to a restaurant tonight.' ....

3 'Let me help you clean your room.' ....

4 'Let's always be best friends.' ....

3 **Circle the correct word.**

She ....eats..... a lot of fruit.

A eat   **(B** eats)   **C** eating

1 Don't talk. You .... be quiet.

A usually   **B** must   **C** mustn't

2 'Do you know Sophie?' 'No, I ....'

A not   **B** aren't   **C** don't

3 Where .... go to school?

A do you   **B** you   **C** you do

4 I .... stay up late on weekdays.

A not   **B** don't   **C** doesn't

5 It's very late. I must .... to bed.

A go   **B** to go   **C** going

6 We like .... to the beach.

A go   **B** we go   **C** going

7 'Does Rose wear glasses?' 'No, she ....'

A isn't   **B** don't   **C** doesn't

8 That cake is for tomorrow. You .... eat it now.

A aren't   **B** must   **C** mustn't

9 '............. like?' 'He's tall with dark hair.'

A What's his   **B** What's he   **C** What is

4 **Correct the underlined words.**

I like skateing. .skating...................

1 You must wearing a jacket today. ....

2 She don't speak French. ....

3 He like playing computer games. ....

4 You doesn't know my cousin. ....

5 **Put the words in order.**

at / do / a lot of / my / school / sports / We
We.do.a.lot.of.sports.at.my.school...........

1 a / in / parents / school / Tara's / work
....

2 brother / in / doesn't / house / helping / the / My / like
....
....

3 be / corridor / in / must / quiet / the / You
....

4 café / Does / in / like / sister / that / working / your / ?
....
....

2

GRAMMAR FILE

let + object pronouns

My parents let me choose my clothes.
Our teacher doesn't let us use a dictionary in tests.
Please let me stay up late tonight, Mum.
Do Jade's parents let her stay out late?
Do Tony's parents let him go surfing on his own?
Jo and Dan's parents don't let them watch TV on weekdays.

- We use *let* to talk about permission. It has the same meaning as *allow* or *permit*.

  let is followed by the base form of the verb – the infinitive without *to*, e.g. *My mum lets me use her computer for my homework.* NOT: ~~My mum lets me to use her computer for my homework.~~

  In the present tense, the negative of *let* is *don't let / doesn't let,* e.g. *Emily's parents don't let her go to the city centre on her own.*

Object pronouns (revision)

You aren't listening to me.
Can I play with you?
Do you know him?
I'm giving this CD to her.
Don't eat it now!
Why are they looking at us?
My parents can take you to the station.
Who are those boys? I often see them at the bus stop.

- We studied object pronouns in Workbook 1, Unit 8 page 89. Now it's time to revise them!
- Object pronouns always come after the verb, e.g. *Do you know her? Please answer me. She always gives us beautiful presents.*
- We also use object pronouns after prepositions, e.g. *I'm going on holiday with her. I don't want to talk to him. I'm making supper for them today. Liam doesn't like playing football with us.*
- We use the object pronoun *them* to talk about people, animals or things in the plural, e.g. *I'm staying with Sabina and Ally. Do you remember them? Where are the hamsters? One of them is in the cage and the other is in my hand. Those are my letters. Please don't read them.*

would like

I'd like a sandwich, please.
Would you like a drink?
What would you like to drink?
Would you like to come to my house for dinner?
I'd like a lemonade and Abby would like a milkshake.

- We use *would like* for offers, invitations, requests and polite responses.
- We can use *would like* with nouns and pronouns, e.g. *Would you like a chocolate? Would your friend like one?* We can also use *would like* with the infinitive, e.g. *Would you like to try one of these sweets?* We do NOT use *would like* with the gerund (*-ing* form), e.g. ~~Would you like trying one of these sweets?~~
- *would* has the same form for all persons.
- We usually use the short form *I'd* in requests, e.g. *I'd like two chocolate ice creams, please.*
- We can't write the short form *'d* in questions, e.g. *What would you like to do tomorrow?* NOT: ~~What'd you like to do tomorrow?~~

How much/many + noun

How much milk do you want in your coffee?
How much money do you get from your parents?
How much tea do you drink every day?
How much time do you spend on your homework?

How many pen-friends have you got?
How many letters do you write a week?
How many sweets are there in the bag?
How many times a week do you go swimming?

- We use *How much* and *How many* to ask questions about quantity.

- We use *How much* with uncountable nouns, like money, time, cheese. For example: *How much money does he spend on clothes? How much time have we got? How much cheese do you want on your spaghetti?*

- We use *How many* with plural countable nouns, like pens, sweets, children. For example: *How many pens are there in the drawer? How many sweets have you got? How many children in your class cycle to school?*

How much is ...? How much are ...?

How much is the blue jacket?
How much are the black trainers?

- We use *How much is / are* to ask the price, e.g. *How much is this tennis racket? How much are these tennis balls?* In these sentences, *How much* means *How much money is this?* or *How much money are these?*

Mum doesn't let me do anything

Vocabulary

1 **What are the names of these shops? Write the letters in the correct order.**

1 j e_ w_ e l l e r 's

2 n _ _ _ _ _ _ _ _ 's

3 d _ _ _ c _ _ _ ss _ n

4 c _ _ _ _ _ 's

5 m _ _ _ _ s _ _ _ _

6 c _ _ _ _ _ _ s _ _ _

7 b _ _ _ _ _

8 d _ _ _ _ _ _ _ _ _ s _ _ _ _

9 b _ _ _ _ _ _ 's

10 s _ _ _ _ _ _ _ _ _ _

11 b _ _ _ _ _

12 s _ _ _ _ _ s _ _ _

Dialogue work

2 **Use the words to complete the dialogue.**

bed	friend	mum	shopping	think
early	late	own	~~strict~~	

Kate Jade's parents are quite ......strict........ .

Sophie Are they?

Kate Yes. They don't let her stay up
(1) .... at weekends.

Sophie What time does she go to
(2) .... on Saturday?

Kate Nine o'clock, I (3) ....

Sophie That's really (4) ....

Kate I know. And they don't let her go
(5) .... on her own.

Sophie I don't like shopping on my
(6) .... I always go with
a (7) ....

Kate But Jade always goes shopping with her
(8) ....

Sophie Poor thing!

Grammar practice

3 Choose the correct word. Complete the sentences.

choose	make	sleep	watch	stay
listen	read	speak	~~use~~	

Do your parents let you ...use..... their computer?

1 My sister doesn't let me .... her diary.

2 Our teacher doesn't let us .... our own language in the English class.

3 Tina's mother lets her .... up until ten.

4 Some parents don't let their children .... TV on weekdays.

5 Does your mother let you .... your own clothes?

6 I don't let my dog .... on my bed.

7 My mother lets me .... cakes.

8 Do you let your sister .... to your CDs?

4 Read what Adam's mother says, then write what Adam says.

> You can't stay up late on weekdays.
>
> You can stay up late at the weekend.
>
> 1 You can't ride your bike to school.
>
> 2 You can ride your bike in the park.
>
> 3 You can't watch TV in the morning.
>
> 4 You can watch TV after school.
>
> 5 You can't cook supper on weekdays.
>
> 6 You can cook supper at the weekend.
>
> 7 You can't play football in the house.
>
> 8 You can play football in the garden.

5 Rewrite the sentences like the examples.

'You mustn't read my e-mails, Tom.'

Tom's mother doesn't let him read her e-mails.

'You can use my computer, Sandra.'

Sandra's father lets her use his computer.

1 'You can listen to the radio in bed.'
My parents ....
....

2 'You mustn't watch TV in the morning, you two.'
Our mother ....
....

3 'You can get up late on Sunday, Beth.'
Beth's mother ....
....

4 'Jo and Ben, you mustn't ride your bikes in the house.'
Their father ....
....

5 'Ricky, you mustn't do your homework in front of the TV.'
Ricky's father ....
....

My mother doesn't let me stay up late on weekdays.

She lets me stay up late at the weekend.

1 ....

2 ....

3 ....
....

4 ....

5 ....
....

6 ....

7 ....
....

8 ....

6 Write questions in the Present simple with *let*.

you / your sister / wear your clothes?
.....Do you let your sister wear your clothes?...
....

1 Tim / his dog / sleep in his room?
....

2 your parents / you cook?
....

3 you / your little brother / come into your room?
....
....

4 your Maths teacher / you / use / calculators?
....
....

7 Dave isn't a very good babysitter. Use the prompts to write his questions and suggestions with *Would you like*?

[e] hot?	**a**	a magazine		Are you hot? Would you like an ice cream? ....
1 [ ] cold?	**b**	your bed	**1**	....
2 [ ] hungry?	**c**	your teddy bear	**2**	....
3 [ ] thirsty?	**d**	a fleece	**3**	....
4 [ ] bored?	**e**	~~an ice cream~~	**4**	....
5 [ ] tired?	**f**	some orange juice	**5**	....
6 [ ] frightened?	**g**	hamburger	**6**	....

8 Complete the dialogue with *would ... like* or *I'd like*.

Dad What ....would....... you ....like......, Amy?

Amy .....I'd like..... a sandwich, please.

Dad What (**1**) .... you .... in your sandwich?

Amy (**2**) .... tuna, please.

Dad OK. And (**3**) .... you .... some orange juice?

Amy No, thanks. Can I have apple juice?

Dad OK. And what about you, Will?

Will (**4**) .... a chicken sandwich.

Dad Anita, what (**5**) .... you ....?

Anita I'm not hungry.

Dad (**6**) .... you .... a drink?

Anita Yes, please. (**7**) .... a milkshake.

Dad Vanilla, chocolate or banana?

Anita (**8**) .... a chocolate milkshake, please.

9 Read the list and write questions with *How much is/are ...?*

SNACKS & DRINKS

Ice cream   Sandwiches
1 Orange juice   4 Apples
2 Fizzy drinks   5 Bananas
3 Hot chocolate   6 Chocolate cake

How much is the ice cream? ....

How much are the sandwiches? ....

1 ....

2 ....

3 ....

4 ....

5 ....

6 ....

10 Complete the *How many ...* questions.

How many days .... are there in a week?

Seven. ....

1 Q: .... are there in the alphabet?

   A: Twenty-six. ....

2 Q: .... hours are there in a day?

   A: Twenty-four. ....

3 Q: .... are there in January?

   A: Thirty-one. ....

4 Q: .... months are there in a ....?

   A: Twelve. ....

11 Complete the questions with *How much* and a word from the box.

| fruit | ~~cheese~~ | money | time | water |

Q: ..How much cheese... do we need?

A: 200 grams.

1 Q: .... do they need?

   A: One hour.

2 Q: ....do you need?

   A: £20.

3 Q: .... do you want?

   A: One litre.

4 Q: .... do you eat a day?

   A: One banana and two apples.

12 Choose the correct word.

How (much /(many) people are there in your family?

1 How (much / many) children are there in your school?

2 How (much / many) pocket money do you get?

3 How (much / many) sweets are there in the packet?

4 How (much / many) water does your dog drink?

5 How (much / many) milk is there in the fridge?

6 How (much / many) apples would you like?

7 How (much / many) time have you got?

8 How (much / many) times a day do you clean your teeth?

13 Write *much* or *many* in the gaps.

A: I want to go to Dizzy's concert.
   How ....much........... are the tickets?

B: They're £15. I can get the tickets for you.
   How ....many......... tickets do you want?

A: Three, please.

A: How (1) .... money have you got?

B: Why?

A: I want those sweets.

B: How (2) .... are they?

A: £1!

A: How (3) .... times a week do you wash your hair?

B: I wash it every day.

A: How (4) .... is your shampoo?

B: £1.50.

A: How (5) .... are the postcards?

B: They're £1.50 for ten. How
   (6) .... postcards do you want?

A: Ten, please.

Culture spot

Pocket money

Money, Money, Money
by Richard Donovan

My parents don't give me pocket money. But I get money from my two **jobs**. There's an old lady in my street called Mrs Drury. She's got a dog called Snoopy. Sometimes Mrs Drury doesn't want to take Snoopy for a walk. So I take him for a nice long walk and Mrs Drury gives me £2. My mum says I mustn't take money from Mrs Drury. But Mrs Drury likes paying me and I can't stop her. And I like taking Snoopy for walks. I usually take him for three walks a week. So I get £6 a week.

My other job is a **newspaper round**. I get £12 a week for that. I get the newspapers from the newsagent. The newsagent gives me a **list**. Then I take the newspapers to all the houses on the list. I don't like that job much. It's boring and the bag of newspapers is very **heavy**. But I like the money! I don't spend my money. I save it. I want to buy a video camera. At the moment I've got £90 in the bank.

My Pocket Money £££
by Maria Hitchcock

I get my pocket money at the weekend. My mum gives me £7 a week. I'd like to get £10 like my friend, Ella. But my mum says no. I usually spend all my money at the weekend on things for my room like posters, **candles**, **incense** and **frames** for all my photos. Sometimes I buy **nail varnish** and **make-up**. I also buy jewellery. I collect **bracelets** and earrings. I've got thirty-three pairs of **earrings** now! Sometimes I save my pocket money for two weeks and buy a CD. CDs are very expensive. They cost about £15. When I want to go to the cinema with friends, my parents pay because it's expensive. My mother also pays for videos. We never buy them. We always **rent videos**. It costs about £4 to rent a new one for the weekend.

1 **Read the text by Richard and answer the questions.**

1 Does Richard get pocket money from his parents?

....

2 What is his job with Mrs Drury?

....

3 How much money does he get a week from her?

....

4 How much does Richard get for his paper round?

....

5 Does he like doing the paper round?

....

6 Does Richard spend his money?

....

7 What does he want to buy?

....

8 How much money has he got in the bank?

....

2 **Read the text by Maria and write T (true) or F (false).**

1 Maria gets her pocket money on Mondays. ......

2 Her friend Ella gets £10 a week. ......

3 Maria collects jewellery. ......

4 Maria buys a CD every week. ......

5 Maria doesn't use her own pocket money for cinema tickets. ......

6 Maria's mother sometimes buys her videos. ......

Vocabulary

3 **Try to guess the meaning of the words. Then check in the dictionary.**

job ....

newspaper round ....

list ....

heavy ....

candles ....

incense ....

frames ....

nail varnish ....

make-up ....

bracelets ....

earrings ....

rent videos ....

Portfolio

4 **Write about your pocket money. Complete the sentences about yourself and delete the unnecessary words.**

POCKET MONEY

- I get .... pocket money a week.

- Sometimes I get money at birthdays and Christmas from ....

    ....

- I *sometimes / never* earn money by working.

- I spend my pocket money on ....

    ....

    ....

- I *sometimes / never* save my pocket money.

- I'm saving up to buy ....

    ....

- I keep my pocket money in ....

    ....

- *I've got / I haven't got* money in the bank.

- I *sometimes / never* borrow money from my *friends / parents*.

- I *always / never* have enough money.

Let's read

What do you do with your pocket money?

1 Read what Jack and Georgia say and complete the chart.

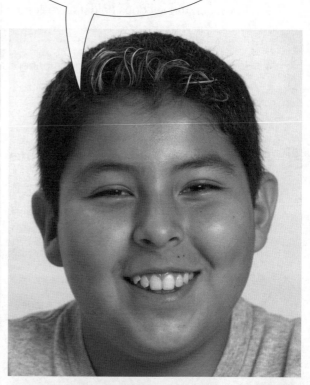

My name's Jack. I'm twelve. I get £10 pocket money a week. I spend about £5 a week on the cinema and cafes and I save £5. I'm saving up for some new computer games. I don't have a weekend job but I help my parents in the house. I tidy my room and clean the bathroom. For my next birthday, I'd like a mobile phone.

	Jack	Georgia
Age?	12	
How much pocket money do they get a week?		
How much do they spend?		
What do they spend their money on?	Going to the cinema and cafés	
How much do they save?		
What are they saving for?		
What jobs do they do at home or for their parents?	Tidies his room and	....
What do they want for their next birthday?		

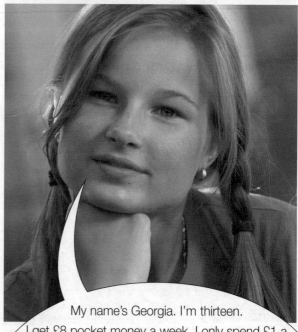

My name's Georgia. I'm thirteen. I get £8 pocket money a week. I only spend £1 a week on my favourite magazine. I'm saving up for a holiday. I want to go skiing with my school next year and my mum says I must pay for the trip with my money. I help my mum with the shopping. We haven't got a car so we go to the supermarket together and I help with the heavy shopping bags. For my next birthday, I'd like ski boots.

Let's check

1 **Match the things you buy with the shops.**

bakery	clothes shop	newsagent's
bookshop	~~music store~~	sports shop
butcher's	jeweller's	supermarket
café	department store	

a CD ..music store...

1 a TV, a dress and a bag.....................................

2 a dictionary ....

3 a magazine ....

4 a shirt ....

5 a watch ....

6 an orange juice and a sandwich ....

7 bread ....

8 cereal, orange juice and shampoo
....

9 chicken and sausages ....

10 trainers and tennis shorts ....

2 **Choose the correct word.**

How much ....is...... that pink diary?

A is   **B** does   **C** are

1 My parents don't let .... cycle to school.

A I   **B** my   **C** me

2 I'd .... a chicken sandwich, please.

A likes   **B** like   **C** liking

3 Don't let .... come into the room.

A he   **B** his   **C** him

4 'I'm thirsty.' '............... you like some juice?'

A Do   **B** Are   **C** Would

5 How .... is this CD?

A many   **B** money   **C** much

6 Aisha doesn't let anyone .... her computer.

A use   **B** using   **C** to use

7 How much .... the postcards?

A is   **B** are   **C** make

8 How .... money have you got?

A much   **B** many   **C** lot

9 How .... sweets are there?

A much   **B** many   **C** lot

10 They never let .... go on the internet.

A we   **B** us   **C** our

3 **Correct the underlined words.**

Would you likes a sandwiches?

Would you like a sandwich?...........................

1 Rosie and Jo's parents never lets they watch TV after school.

....

....

2 How much sweet have you got in your bag?

....

....

3 How much are this boxes of chocolates?

....

....

4 How many sugar does you want in your tea?

....

....

5 I am like two ticket for the film at four, please.

....

....

4 **Choose the correct word.**

How (much / many) bananas do you want?

1 How (much / many) time do you spend on homework?

2 How (much / many) are these pink socks?

3 How (much / many) money have you got with you?

4 How (much / many) is a tuna sandwich?

5 How (much / many) cheese do you want on your pasta?

Extra!

1 Complete A's part of the dialogue.

Read the whole dialogue before you start writing the missing part.

Don't just read the sentences that come before the gaps. The sentences that follow the gaps are often more useful.

A: Have you got any brothers or sisters?

B: Yes, I've got a brother and a sister.

A: ....?

B: My brother is sixteen and my sister is fourteen.

A: ....?

B: My brother? He's quite tall and he's very good at sport.

A: ....?

B: My sister's name is Karen.

A: ....?

B: Yes, she does. She loves music.

A: ....
....?

B: Her favourite bands are *Coldplay* and *Oasis*.

A: ....?

B: No, she can't but I can. In fact, I play the guitar in a band.

A: Really?...?

B: It's called the *Blue Electrix*.

A: ....?

B: We play at school discos and concerts.

A: ....?

B : Yes, I like sport, but I prefer music.

A: ....
....?

B: I like football and tennis.

2 Write a letter to a pen-friend. Answer these questions in your letter:

- Where do you live?
- How old are you?
- How many brothers and sisters have you got? Give their names and ages.
- Describe your family. What are your parents, brother(s) and/or sister(s) like?
- What is your favourite subject at school?
- What are your hobbies?
- What do you usually do at the weekend?

Ask these questions:

- What does your pen-friend like doing in his/her free time?
- What are his/her favourite bands?
- Has he/she got a favourite football team? What is it?

Sign your letter.
Write between 100 and 120 words.

Dear

....
....
....
....
....
....
....
....
....
....
....
....
....
....
....
....
....
....
....
....

Please write to me soon.

3 Match the descriptions to the places. There are two extra places.

1 People change money here. ....

2 You can buy meat here. ....

3 You buy newspapers and magazines here.
....

4 This shop has bread and cakes. ....

5 You can buy a necklace or watch here.
....

bakery	chemist's
bank	jeweller's
butcher's	newsagent's
~~café~~	supermarket

4 Complete the five dialogues. Circle A, B or C.

0 Where do you come from?
 A The park.
 B Poland.
 C On the bus.

1 What's she like?
 A Yes, I like her.
 B She liked it a lot.
 C Quite shy.

2 Can I help you?
 A Yes, please.
 B No, don't.
 C Yes, you must.

3 Which one would you like?
 A No, thanks.
 B The blue one.
 C I like them.

4 What are you doing here?
 A I'm not doing it.
 B Shopping.
 C Fine, thanks.

5 How much is that poster?
 A I've got three.
 B It's very nice.
 C Six euros.

5 Complete the sentences about Finn's school day with the correct word. Circle A, B or C.

EXAMPLE

0 Finn usually .gets. up at half past seven.
 A starts **B** gets **C** stands

1 He … to school at eight fifteen.
 A meets **B** goes **C** arrives

2 He … grey trousers and a tie for school.
 A puts **B** clothes **C** wears

3 He sometimes has a … to eat at break.
 A food **B** sandwich **C** apple

4 His … subject is Maths.
 A likes **B** especially **C** favourite

5 Finn's mother doesn't … him stay up late on school days.
 A let **B** allow **C** want

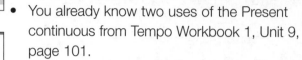

GRAMMAR FILE

Present continuous as future

Affirmative

I'm leaving tomorrow.
You're leaving tomorrow.
She's/He's/It's leaving tomorrow.
We're/You're/They're leaving tomorrow.

Negative

I'm not leaving on Saturday.
You aren't leaving on Saturday.
She/He/It isn't leaving on Saturday.
We/You/They aren't leaving on Saturday.

Questions

Am I leaving in the morning?
Are you leaving in the morning?
Is she/he/it leaving in the morning?
Are we/you/they leaving in the morning?

- You already know two uses of the Present continuous from Tempo Workbook 1, Unit 9, page 101.
  – We use the Present continuous for actions which are happening now, at the moment when we are speaking, e.g. *Why is Milly talking to the mirror? She's practising for her audition!*
  – We also use it to talk about actions which are happening during the present period, e.g. *Is your team doing well this year? Are you winning a lot of games?*

- We also use the Present continuous to talk about fixed arrangements for the future, especially when we say the time and place, e.g. *I'm meeting Annabel at the bus stop at four. Bashir isn't coming to the party on Saturday. What time is the taxi coming tomorrow?*

- We form the Present continuous with the present of the verb *be* + the present participle of the verb (*listening, watching, writing, running, sitting*).
  There are spelling rules for forming the present participle. Here are some of them:
  We usually add *ing* to the verb, e.g. *go – going, work – working*.
  If a verb ends in one *e*, we take away the *e* and add *ing*, e.g. *come – coming, write – writing*.
  If a verb has a short vowel and ends in one consonant, we double the consonant, e.g. *run – running, sit –sitting, swim – swimming, shop – shopping*.

Short answers

Affirmative	Negative
Yes, I am.	No, I'm not.
Yes, you are.	No, you aren't.
Yes, she/he/it is.	No, she/he/it isn't.
Yes, we/you/they are.	No, we/you/they aren't.

- We always use the long form of the verb *be* in affirmative short answers: *Are you playing in the match on Saturday? Yes, I am.*
  NOT: ~~Yes, I'm.~~

Future with *going to*

Affirmative
I'm going to help.
You're going to help.
She's/He's/It's going to help.
We're/You're/They're going to help.

Negative
I'm not going to be late.
You aren't going to be late.
She/He/It isn't going to be late.
We/you/They aren't going to be late.

Questions
Am I going to be ready?
Are you going to be ready?
Is she/he/it going to be ready?
Are we/you/they going to be ready?

Short answers

Affirmative	**Negative**
Yes, I am.	No, I'm not.
Yes, she/he/it is.	No, she/he/it isn't.
Yes, we/you/they are.	No, we/you/they aren't.

- We use *going to* to talk about a planned future action, e.g. *I'm going to buy some new jeans this weekend. What are you going to wear to the party?*
- We also use *going to* to talk about something we can predict because of what is happening now, e.g. *The sky is black. It's going to rain. Our team is playing really well. We're going to win the match.*

- The future with *going to* is formed with the Present continuous of *go* + *to* + the base form of the verb, e.g. *I am going to leave. We aren't going to stay. What are you going to do?*

- We always use the long form of the verb *be* in affirmative short answers: *Are you going to wear your new T-shirt to the party? Yes, I am.* NOT: *Yes, I'm. Is Sylvie going to be there? Yes, she is.* NOT: *Yes, she's.*

Want + infinitive

Affirmative
I want to leave.
Negative
I don't want to stay.
Questions
Do you want to go?
Does he want to come with us?
What do they want to do?

- *want* can be followed by a noun or pronoun, e.g. *I want a sandwich. Do you want one?* It can also be followed by the infinitive, e.g. *They want to go out. What do you want to do?*
- Be careful! It isn't correct to say *I want. / I don't want*. We have to say *I want to / I don't want to*. For example, *Let's go swimming. I don't want to. Why are you wearing that hat? Because I want to.*

Suggestions: *Let's, Why don't we*

Let's go swimming.
Why don't we stay at home and watch a video?

- We can make suggestions with *Let's* + the base form of the verb, e.g. *Let's have lunch in the garden.*
- *Let's* is the short form of *Let us*.
- We can also make suggestions with *Why don't we* + the base form of the verb, eg. *Why don't we watch a video?*

3

What are we doing at the weekend?

Vocabulary

1 **Write what the weather is like next to each picture. Choose the words from the box.**

cloudy	~~hot and sunny~~	snowing
foggy	raining	windy

1  It's hot and sunny.

2  ....

3 ....

4 ....

5 ....

6  ....

Dialogue work

2 **Complete the dialogues with the sentences below.**

Anna	Are you doing anything at the weekend?
Dan	*Yes, I'm going to the beach with Rose.*
Anna	Is that on Saturday or Sunday?
Dan	(1) ....
Anna	So what are you doing on Saturday?
Dan	(2) ....
Anna	My mum's taking us to a theme park.
Dan	(3) ....
Anna	Why don't you come too?
Dan	(4) ....

- Lucky you!
- Nothing, really. What about you?
- Sunday.
- Thanks. That sounds great!
- ~~Yes. I'm going to the beach with Rose.~~

Mum	Where are you going?
Kate	(5) ....
Mum	Where?
Kate	(6) ....
Mum	You're going to be late.
Kate	(7) ....
Mum	Wait a minute.
Kate	(8) ....
Mum	It's going to rain. Take this umbrella.
Kate	(9) ....
Mum	Are you coming home for lunch?
Kate	(10) ....
Mum	OK, darling. Have fun.

- I don't know. Why don't I phone you?
- I know. Bye.
- Outside *Juice Box*.
- Shopping with Alice. I'm meeting her at ten.
- Thanks, Mum.
- What is it now?

Grammar practice

3 Choose the correct verb and write it in the Present continuous.

not play	sleep	snow
do	not wear	stay
not rain	sing	not watch

Be quiet! I'm doing.. my Maths and it's really difficult.

1 It .... now. We can go out and play in the park.

2 It .... The garden is all white.

3 I .... rubbish on TV. It's a very good programme.

4 I can't read the board. I .... my glasses.

5 Jade isn't here. She .... at a friend's house.

6 Listen! She .... a French song.

7 I .... very well. I can't get the ball.

8 Sandra .... She's very tired after the trip.

4 Write questions in the Present continuous. Then match each one to the correct answer.

(it / rain) again?

Is it raining again? .... [f]

1 Why (you / wear) that ridiculous hat?

.... [ ]

....

2 Who (Sandra / talk to) on the phone?

.... [ ]

3 (your parents / do) the garden at the moment?

.... [ ]

....

4 (Jack / write) a postcard to Selina?

.... [ ]

5 What (Cath / read) at the moment?

.... [ ]

a) Another Harry Potter book.

b) Because I like it.

c) Her mother, I think.

d) No, he isn't. It's to Lucy.

e) No, they're making the lunch.

f) Yes, it is.

5 Put the verbs in the Present continuous.

Dear Millie

The birds .....are singing...... (sing) and it's a beautiful day. I (1).......................... (write) this postcard on the beach. Josh and Dan (2)...............
.... (play) football and Serena
(3).......................... (swim). Anita
(4).......................... (wear) her new sunglasses. She thinks she's very cool! Tom
(5).......................... (eat) his fourth ice cream!!!
Joey and Stacey (6)..........................
(sit) under the beach umbrella. They (7)..........................
.... (listen) to CDs. What
(8).......................... (you / do) in London?
(9).......................... (you / study)
for your exams? You poor thing! (10)..........................
.... (Mark / still work) in the
bookshop? Write to me. Love Lisa

6 Look at Ben's diary for the weekend and write sentences in the Present continuous.

Saturday
morning: play tennis
afternoon: do homework YUCK!!
evening: go to cinema with Rob
Sunday
morning: clean Dad's car ⊥⊥⊥!!
afternoon: help Mum with party food
evening: have party at my house YES!!

On Saturday morning ..he's playing tennis...........

1 On Saturday afternoon ....
....

2 On Saturday evening ....
....

3 On Sunday morning ....
....

4 On Sunday afternoon ....
....

5 On Sunday evening ....
....

3

7 **Write sentences in the Present continuous. Then choose the response.**

I'm playing. (play) in a match tomorrow. [d]

1 Where .... (you / have) your birthday party? [ ]

2 I .... (not / do) anything special at the weekend. [ ]

3 I .... (not / take) the dog for a walk tonight. [ ]

4 .... (they / drive) to the beach or .... (they / take) the bus? [ ]

5 What .... (you / give) Rose for her birthday? [ ]

a) A jewellery box.
b) Are you very tired?
c) At Great Scots. It's a cool restaurant.
d) ~~Good luck!~~
e) They're driving.
f) Why don't you come round to my house?

8 **Put the verbs in these pairs of sentences in the future with *going to*.**

I (not / make) supper tonight.

I'm not going to make supper tonight.

I (go) to bed early.

I'm going to go to bed early.

1 We (not / have) a picnic this weekend.

....

We (have) one next weekend.

....

2 Dad (not / buy) a new computer.

....

He (use) his old one.

....

3 Emma and Clare (not / see) the new film at the ABC Cinema.

....

....

They (watch) a video at home.

....

4 You (not / like) this CD.

....

In fact, you (hate) it.

....

5 I (not / take) a sweater.

....

It (be) really hot this afternoon.

....

9 **Complete the captions using *(not) going to*. Include a verb from the list below in each caption.**

| eat | fall | ~~rain~~ |
| make | say | win |

It's going to rain. Take your umbrella.

1 I don't like this food and I .... it.

2 Our team is really bad today. We ....

3 They ....
.... snowman.

4 Please listen everyone because I ....
.... this again.

5 Look. He ....
.... in.

ANGING ROOMS

Mrs Campbell Kate's going to make dinner tonight.

Mr Campbell What (6) ....?

Mrs Campbell Lasagne and salad, I think.

Mr Campbell I'm hungry. When (7) ....
.... make it?

Mrs Campbell She's going to start in about five minutes.

(11) Use the prompts to write suggestions with *Why don't we* and *Let's*.

	Josie	go to the cinema?
	Andy	watch a video?
1	Jack	have dinner?
	Tara	have a drink.
2	Suzy	watch TV?
	Jen	go out.
3	Dan	go for a bike ride?
	Luke	go skating?
4	Amy	make a pizza?
	Joey	buy one.
5	Ryan	listen to the radio?
	Rob	listen to a CD?

Josie Why don't we go to the cinema?...

Andy No let's watch a video....................

1 **Jack** ....

Tara No, ...

2 **Suzy** ....

Jen No, ...

3 **Dan** ....

Luke No, ...

4 **Amy** ....

Joey No, ...

5 **Ryan** ....

Rob No, ...

(10) Complete the questions in these conversations. Use the future with *going to.*

Kate I'm going to meet some friends.

Mum Who are you going to meet.........?

Kate Emily and Ashan.

Mum Where (1) .... them?

Kate At the Net Café.

Mum Why (2) .... them there?

Kate Because it's a nice café.

Alex I'm going to buy some new trainers this weekend.

Ashan Which ones (3) ....?

Alex I'm not sure yet.

Ashan Where (4) .... them?

Alex At the new sport shop in Clayton Street.

Ashan Why (5) .... them there?

Alex Because it's a really good shop.

Read

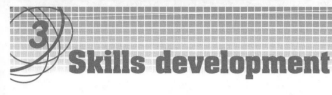

Carnival time!

On Saturday my friend Charmaine and I are going to be in a dance **group** at the Notting Hill Carnival. It's a huge Caribbean carnival with Caribbean music and dancing. It's at the end of August every year and it's always fantastic. It's a big street party in an **area** of London called Notting Hill.

It goes on for three days <u>Saturday, Sunday and Monday</u> . Everybody sings and dances in the street. **Lorries** drive down the streets with bands and dancers in amazing **costumes**. You can buy delicious Caribbean food (**1**)............................... ....

Charmaine is coming round to my house quite early on Saturday. Then we're going to (**2**)............... ....

at Mei Lin's house. Mei Lin is a really clever woman and she's making the costumes for all the people (**3**) .... Our costumes are **amazing**. (**4**)............................. .... At one o'clock we're going to get on the lorry with the band and we're going to parade (**5**)....................... .... We're going to sing and dance and the band is going to play Caribbean music. **Thousands** of people are going to watch us! My parents are going to be there, of course. I'm a bit nervous but (**6**)... .

by Davina Thomas

1 **Read the article. Where should these phrases go?**

a) get dressed for the parade

b) I'm really looking forward to it

c) I'm a blue bird and Charmaine's a green parrot

d) in our dance group

e) like spicy barbecued chicken and cooked bananas

f) ~~Saturday, Sunday and Monday~~

g) through the streets

2 **Read the text again and translate these words. If you don't know them, guess and then check in a dictionary or with your teacher.**

group ....

area ....

lorries ....

costumes ....

amazing ....

thousands ....

....

....

....

....

....

....

....

....

....

....

....

....

....

....

....

Write

3 **You're going to a carnival with a friend. Write what you're planning to do there. Start like this:**

I'm going to meet my friend ....

at ....

We're going to ....

....

There's going to be ....

....

....

It's going to be fun because ....

....

....

Study tips

4 **It's a good idea to use English in the classroom as much as possible. Put these words in order, to make some useful classroom phrases.**

1 please / Can / that / you / repeat / ?

....

2 do / How / *Notting Hill* / spell / you / ?

....

3 do / pronounce / you / How / word / this / ?

....

4 does / mean / this / What / word / ?

....

3 Talk time

1 Put the sentences in order, to make a dialogue.

- And how much are those little boxes?
- ~~Can I help you?~~
- Here's 5 pounds.
- I'd like two boxes please.
- It's 7 pounds.
- Thank you. Here's your change.
- That's 4 pounds, please.
- They're 2 pounds each.
- ~~Yes, please. How much is that baseball cap?~~

Assistant		Can I help you?
Customer		Yes, please. How much is that baseball cap?
Assistant	1	
Customer	2	
Assistant	3	
Customer	4	
Assistant	5	
Customer	6	
Assistant	7	

2 Write the phrases in the correct balloons.

- I want to go to the cinema.
- Let's go surfing.
- Why don't we play football?

Let's check

1 **Complete the sentences with these words.**

cool	foggy	raining	thunder
cold	lightning	snowing	~~warm~~

It's cold today but this jacket is nice and ....**warm**..

1 Winters in Sweden are very ....

2 It's .... Let's make a snowman.

3 It's .... Take an umbrella.

4 It's very hot in the sun. But under this tree, it's nice and ....

5 You mustn't drive fast. It's .... and you can't see the street.

6 My cat is frightened of .... and .... She doesn't like storms.

2 **Choose the correct words.**

What .....**are**...... you doing at the weekend?

A do   **B** are ⟲   **C** does

1 I'm .... to wear my new jeans to the party.

A go   **B** think   **C** going

2 Let's .... to the beach on Sunday.

A go   **B** going   **C** to go

3 Why .... play tennis tomorrow?

A we aren't   **B** we don't   **C** don't we

4 Be quiet. I'm .... my homework.

A do   **B** doing   **C** going to

5 They don't want .... swimming.

A going   **B** go   **C** to go

3 **Write the sentences in the Present continuous. Do they refer to the present (P) or the future (F)?**

........**I'm going**........ (I / go) to the beach tomorrow with James.   [F]

1 .... (Andrea / not wear) her new jeans to the party on Saturday.   [ ]

2 Why .... (you / eat) my chicken, you naughty cat?   [ ]

3 Really Miss Corden, ... (I / not draw) on the desk.   [ ]

4 .... (Who / make) a cake for Sam's birthday next week?   [ ]

5 .... (I get) bored with this music. Let's change it.   [ ]

4 **Correct the mistakes.**

What <u>do</u> you doing in the kitchen?
<u>What are you doing in the kitchen?</u>

1 Let's <u>watching</u> your new video.

....

2 We <u>wants</u> to <u>going</u> out now.

....

3 We <u>don't</u> going to <u>inviting</u> him to our party.

....

4 <u>Which</u> time <u>does</u> she leaving?

....

5 **Put the words in order.**

an / going / It's / rain / take / to / umbrella / so.
<u>It's going to rain so take an umbrella</u>..............

1 Are / the beach / friends / going / to / today / your / ? ....
....

2 are / brother's / letter / reading / Why / you / your / ? ....
....

3 afternoon / friends / I'm / in / meeting / my / this / town

....
....

4 anything / Are / at / doing / the / weekend / you / ?

....
....

GRAMMAR FILE

Future with *will* for offers, predictions and decisions

Affirmative

Long form	Short form
I will stay.	I'll stay.
You will stay.	You'll stay.
She/He/It will stay.	She'll/He'll/It'll stay.
We will stay.	We'll stay.
You will stay.	You'll stay.
They will stay.	They'll stay.

Negative

Long form	Short form
I will not go.	I won't go.
You will not go.	You won't go.
She/He/It will not go.	She/He/It won't go.
We will not go.	We won't go.
You will not go.	You won't go.
They will not go.	They won't go.

Questions

Will I play?
Will you play?
Will she/he/it play?
Will we play?
Will you play?
Will they play?

Short answers

Affirmative	Negative
Yes, I will.	No, I won't.
Yes, you will.	No, you won't.
Yes, she/he/it will.	No, she/he/it won't.
Yes, we will.	No, we won't.
Yes, you will.	No, you won't.
Yes, they will.	No, they won't.

- We can use *will* to make offers, e.g. *We'll take you to the station. I'll help you with your project.*
- We can use *will* and *won't* for decisions, e.g. *I'll leave my bags at the hotel. We won't get the early bus.*
- We can use *will* and *won't* for predictions – to say what we think will happen, e.g. *You'll love Mexico. The weather will be perfect. It won't be cold. Rosa will meet you at the airport.*
- *Will* and *won't* have the same form for all persons.

- When we are writing, we use the affirmative short form *'ll* after pronouns but not after nouns. We write *She'll be sorry* but we don't write *Cath'll be sorry* or *Dave'll know the answer.*

should

Affirmative
I should stop.
You should stop.
She/he/it should stop.
We should stop.
You should stop.
They should stop.

Negative
I shouldn't do it.
You shouldn't do it.
She/he/it shouldn't do it.
We shouldn't do it.
You shouldn't do it.
They shouldn't do it.

Questions
Should I start?
Should you start?
Should she/he/it start?
Should we start?
Should you start?
Should they start?

Short answers

Affirmative	Negative
Yes, I should.	No, I shouldn't.
Yes, you should.	No, you shouldn't.
Yes, she/he/it should.	No, she/he/it shouldn't.
Yes, we should.	No, we shouldn't.
Yes, you should.	No, you shouldn't.
Yes, they should.	No, they shouldn't.

- We use *should* and *shouldn't* to give advice, e.g. *You should take a jumper. It'll be cold in the evening. You shouldn't stay up late tonight. You've got an exam tomorrow.*
- We also use *should* and *shouldn't* to give opinions about what is right or wrong, e.g. *People should recycle paper. You shouldn't drop litter.*
- *must/mustn't* are stronger than *should/ shouldn't*.
- *should/shouldn't* has the same form for all persons.

Possessive pronouns

Subject pronouns	Possessive adjectives	Possessive pronouns
I	my	mine
you	your	yours
she	her	hers
he	his	his
we	our	ours
you	your	yours
they	their	theirs

- We use the possessive adjectives *my, your, her, his, its, our, their* with a noun, e.g. *My fingers are cold. Is this your money? Rosa is wearing her green earrings. I'm putting the hamster in its cage. Their party is on Friday, our party is on Saturday.*
- We use the possessive pronouns *mine, yours, hers, his, ours, theirs* without a noun: *Is this pen mine or yours? Give this to Mark. It's his. Can we have those photos? They're ours.*
- *his* can be a possessive pronoun or a possessive adjective. *This is his jacket.* (his = possessive adjective) *It's his.* (his = possessive pronoun)
- *its* is only a possessive adjective. There isn't an equivalent possessive pronoun.
- We use the question word *Whose* to find out who is the owner of something, e.g. *Whose are these socks? They're mine.*

4

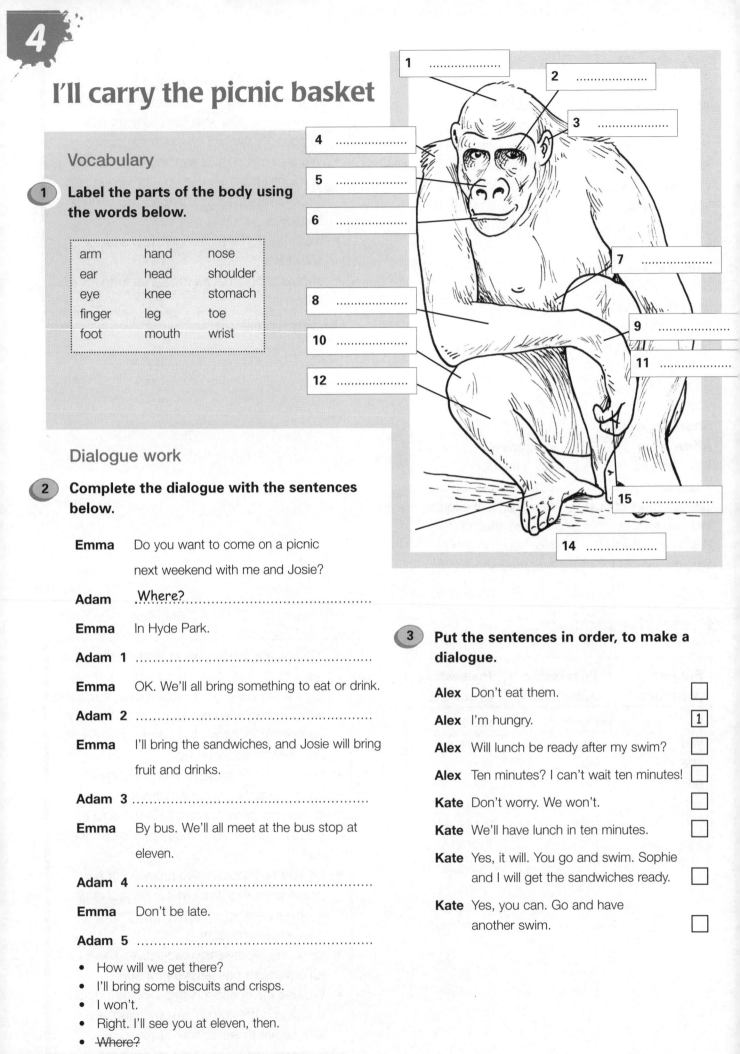

I'll carry the picnic basket

Vocabulary

1. **Label the parts of the body using the words below.**

arm	hand	nose
ear	head	shoulder
eye	knee	stomach
finger	leg	toe
foot	mouth	wrist

1 ....
2 ....
3 ....
4 ....
5 ....
6 ....
7 ....
8 ....
9 ....
10 ....
11 ....
12 ....
14 ....
15 ....

Dialogue work

2. **Complete the dialogue with the sentences below.**

Emma Do you want to come on a picnic next weekend with me and Josie?

Adam Where?...

Emma In Hyde Park.

Adam 1 ....

Emma OK. We'll all bring something to eat or drink.

Adam 2 ....

Emma I'll bring the sandwiches, and Josie will bring fruit and drinks.

Adam 3 ....

Emma By bus. We'll all meet at the bus stop at eleven.

Adam 4 ....

Emma Don't be late.

Adam 5 ....

- How will we get there?
- I'll bring some biscuits and crisps.
- I won't.
- Right. I'll see you at eleven, then.
- ~~Where?~~
- Yes, please!

3. **Put the sentences in order, to make a dialogue.**

Alex Don't eat them. ☐

Alex I'm hungry. [1]

Alex Will lunch be ready after my swim? ☐

Alex Ten minutes? I can't wait ten minutes! ☐

Kate Don't worry. We won't. ☐

Kate We'll have lunch in ten minutes. ☐

Kate Yes, it will. You go and swim. Sophie and I will get the sandwiches ready. ☐

Kate Yes, you can. Go and have another swim. ☐

Grammar practice

4 **Write sentences with *I'll* for each situation, using the prompts.**

- get you a dictionary
- get a sweater for you
- lend you my mobile phone
- make a sandwich for you
- help you with the food
- pay for your ticket
- ~~teach you~~

Your friend:

can't snowboard

I'll teach you.

1 hasn't got any money but wants to go to the cinema

....

2 is very hungry

....

3 wants to phone her mother

....

4 is having a big party

....

5 is very cold

....

6 doesn't understand a difficult word

....

5 **Complete the sentences with *'ll* or *will* and the correct verb. Where possible use *'ll*.**

be	~~give~~	close
carry	have	tidy
get	meet	write

I 'll give...... you the money for the tickets tomorrow.

1 We........................ you at the station at six.

2 Are you thirsty? Dave .... you a drink.

3 I .... a letter to Julia tomorrow.

4 Take your jacket. It .... cold in the park.

5 Give me your bag. I .... it for you.

6 You .... a great time in Scotland.

7 I .... my room at the weekend.

8 Are you cold? I .... the window.

6 **Complete the sentences with the correct possessive pronoun.**

Is this my orange juice?

No, ...**yours**.......... is in the green glass.

1 Is this your fleece?

No, ... has my name in it.

2 Is this Caroline's hat?

No, ... is pink and white.

3 Is this Tim's jacket?

No, ... is on the chair.

4 Is this your parents' computer?

No, it isn't .... It's mine.

5 Jo and Dan, are these your CDs?

No, they aren't .... They're Tina's.

6 Are these my sunglasses?

No, they aren't. .... are in your school bag.

7 **Use the prompts to write pairs of sentences with *'ll* and *won't*.**

We (not / be) late. We (be) back at ten.

We won't be late. We'll be back at ten.

1 I (not / eat) now. There (be) food at the party.

....

....

2 Dan (not / be) angry. He (laugh).

....

3 You (not / lose) the match. You (win)!

....

4 We (not / leave). We (wait) for you.

....

5 Amy (not / phone). She (send) an e-mail.

....

....

6 You (not / like) this video. You (be) frightened.

....

8 **Use the prompts to write questions with *will* and short form answers.**

James / be at the party?

Will James be at the party?

Yes, he will.

1 Suzy / have Max's phone number?

....

No, ...

2 we / get homework tomorrow?

....

Yes, ...

3 it / snow tomorrow?

....

No, ...

4 your parents / tell mine?

....

No, ...

5 you / write to me?

....

Yes, ...

9 **Complete the conversation with the correct form of the future with *will*.**

Alex I'm going camping in Dorset with Joey. Do you want to come too?

Ashan You bet! ..Will we go... (we / go) by train?

Alex Yes, ..we will.. (we ...). And we..'ll take..... (take) our bikes with us. It ..won't be.......... (not / be) difficult.

Ashan Where (**1**) .... (we / camp)?

Alex There's a great campsite at Lulworth near the beach.

Ashan So (**2**) .... (we / go) swimming every day?

Alex Yes, (**3**) .... (we ....). And in the evenings, (**4**)........................ (we / make) our own dinner.

Ashan (**5**) .... (it / be) cold in the evenings?

Alex No, (**6**) .... (it ...). It (**7**) .... (be) nice and warm.

Ashan How much (**8**) .... (the campsite / cost)?

Alex I don't know. I (**9**) .... (ask) my brother. He (**10**) .... (know). But I'm sure it (**11**) .... (not / be) a lot.

Ashan Have you got a tent?

Alex No. We (**12**) .... (use) my brother's. It's for three people.

Ashan Great! So I (**13**) .... (not / need) a tent.

Alex No, you (**14**) .... (not ...).

10 **Complete the advice with *should* or *shouldn't*.**

THE DOCTORS SAY...

You ......should............... drink six glasses of water a day.

1 You .... eat lots of fruit and vegetables.

2 You .... drink a lot of tea and coffee at night.

3 You .... clean your teeth three times a day.

4 You .... eat a lot of sweets, chocolate or sugar.

5 You .... do sport three times a week.

6 You .... eat a good breakfast.

7 You .... stay up late.

8 You .... get eight hours sleep every night.

9 You .... wear sunscreen and a hat to protect you from the sun.

10 You .... sit in the sun in the middle of the day.

11 **Give advice for each situation using** *should* **or** *shouldn't* **and a phrase from the box.**

```
• drink coffee            • sit in the sun all day
• get a Saturday job      • read a good book
• go to bed early         • wear her glasses
```

Louise can't see the blackboard.

She should wear her glasses.

1 Your mother can't sleep.

....

2 Your friend Tony is very tired.

....

3 Your father is sunburnt.

....

4 Lydia doesn't have any money.

....

5 Your sister is bored.

....

12 **Use the prompts to write questions with** *should*. **Then write answers.**

Q: we walk or take a bus?
A: take a bus
1 Q: What / I do with this money?
A: take it to the police station
2 Q: Where / they leave their jackets?
A: in the hall
3 Q: we / answer all the questions?
A: no
4 Q: When / my father come and get me?
A: nine o'clock
5 Q: she / go to the doctor about her leg?
A: yes

Q: *Should we walk or take a bus?*
A: *You should take a bus.*

1 Q: ....

....

A: ....

....

2 Q: ....

....

A: ....

....

3 Q: ....

....

A: ....

....

4 Q: ....

....

A: ....

....

5 Q: ....

....

A: ....

13 **Write questions with** *Whose* **and answers.**

Whose is the .... apple?

It's Alice's.

Whose are the .... pencils?

They're Mark's.

1 .... pens?

....

2 .... calculator?

....

3 .... diary?

....

4 .... crisps?

....

5 .... sunglasses?

....

6 .... frisbee?

....

Culture spot

Edinburgh

Hi Sandro!

I'm having a great time in Scotland and SURPRISE SURPRISE it isn't raining today! We're in Edinburgh at the moment. (You pronounce Edinburgh ed – in – ba – ra, by the way.) There's lots to see and do here. Edinburgh Castle is my favourite place. It's really old! The oldest part of it is about 900 years old. The castle stands on a big **rock** and there's a brilliant **view** of Edinburgh from it. There's an old **gun** outside the castle. At one o'clock every day (**except** Sunday) there's a big BANG from this gun. Then everyone in Edinburgh looks at their watch to check the time!

Prince's Street has the best shops in Edinburgh. I'm going to buy a **tartan scarf** there tomorrow. Nearly all the shops in Prince's Street have got tartan things – tartan trousers, tartan skirts, tartan shirts. I like listening to the **pipers** in Prince's Street. They wear a **kilt** and they play Scottish music on their **bagpipes**.

The Edinburgh Festival is on at the moment. It's the biggest festival of music and theatre in Europe. Every day there are hundreds of **shows**, concerts and dances. Some actors and musicians do their shows in the street. The **atmosphere** is amazing.

Are you having a good time with your grandparents in Sicily? Write to me!

Bye James

1 [...]

2 [...]

3 [...]

1 Read the letter and match the captions to the photos.

a) Edinburgh Castle stands on a big rock.

b) During the Edinburgh Festival you can watch shows in the streets.

c) This is a Scottish piper. He's wearing a kilt and playing the bagpipes.

2 Some words don't have a translation. For example, the English for *spaghetti* and *pasta* is *spaghetti* and *pasta*. Read the definition of *pasta*.

> pasta – Italian food. You make it with flour. You cook it in water and eat it with sauce.

Write definitions of these Scottish words.

1 tartan ....
....

2 kilt ....
....

3 bagpipes ....
....

3 Guess the meaning of these words. Then check in a dictionary.

rock ....

view ....

gun ....

except ....

scarf ....

show ....

atmosphere ....

Portfolio

4 Write about yourself. Tick (✓) the things you will probably do in your next holiday.

Go sightseeing?	[ ]
Take photos?	[ ]
Write postcards?	[ ]
Try different food?	[ ]
Visit historic buildings?	[ ]
Go shopping?	[ ]
Go to a play or concert?	[ ]
Go to a festival?	[ ]
Go to a museum?	[ ]
Meet some new people?	[ ]
Do some sport?	[ ]
Go to the beach?	[ ]

Complete the sentences.

In my next holidays I will probably ....
....
....

I'll probably also ....
....
....

and ....
....
....
....
....
....
....
....
....
....
....
....
....

Let's read

Do girls ever wear kilts?

1 Read the conversation and tick (✓) the things Lauren and Hamish talk about.

1) ☐ Scottish dancing		**6)** ☐ the view
2) ☐ the weather		**7)** ☐ dictionaries
3) ☐ horses		**8)** ☐ Scottish words
4) ☐ history		**9)** ☐ trousers
5) ☐ singing		**10)** ☐ a video

Hamish: So Lauren, what do you think of Scotland?

Lauren: It's great. I'm having a brilliant holiday.

Hamish: Where are you from in the States?

Lauren: I'm from Texas.

Hamish: Are you enjoying the party?

Lauren: Yes. It's fun. But some of these Scottish dances are really fast and I get quite tired!

Hamish: It rains a lot here, doesn't it!

Lauren: I know. But I didn't come to Scotland for the sun. I get plenty of it in Texas!

Hamish: What do you like best about Scotland?

Lauren: I like learning about the past, about all your kings and queens. And I love all the old castles.

Hamish: What do you think of our countryside?

Lauren: I love it. Just look out of the window. Look at those mountains and that beautiful lake.

Hamish: It's not a lake.

Lauren: What do you mean?

Hamish: It's a loch. L- O- C- H. That's the Scottish for a lake.

Lauren: Really? So you don't speak English in Scotland?

Hamish: Of course, we do. But some words are a bit different.

Lauren: Do girls ever wear kilts?

Hamish: Kilts are for men really. But some girls wear them.

Lauren:: Do you wear your kilt every day? I mean do you wear it to school, for example?

Hamish: You're joking. Of course, I don't. Nobody wears a kilt to school. Kilts are just for parties and dances. Do you want to come and dance now? Or do you want to come and see the ghost?

Lauren: What? Is there a ghost in this house?

Hamish: There certainly is. It's in the kitchen.

Lauren: You have your own ghost! That's so cool!

2 Read the conversation again and write T (true) or F (false).

1 Lauren likes Scotland. ☐

2 Lauren is English. ☐

3 Scottish dances are always slow. ☐

4 Lauren likes the Scottish countryside. ☐

5 Loch is the Scottish word for beautiful. ☐

6 Most Scottish boys wear a kilt every day. ☐

7 Hamish says there's a ghost in the house. ☐

Let's check

1 **Match the parts of the body to the things you wear.**

eyes	[b]	**a)** bag
1 feet	[ ]	**b)** ~~glasses~~
2 head	[ ]	**c)** hat
3 legs	[ ]	**d)** shoes
4 shoulder	[ ]	**e)** trousers
5 wrist	[ ]	**f)** watch

2 **Number the parts of the body in the order of their position on the body. Start with the highest part and end with the lowest part.**

a)	finger	[ ]	**f)** nose	[ ]
b)	eyes	[1]	**g)** shoulder	[ ]
c)	knee	[ ]	**h)** stomach	[ ]
d)	mouth	[ ]	**i)** toes	[ ]
e)	neck	[ ]		

3 **Choose the correct words.**

Liam will ..**make**..... the sandwiches.

A making   **B** make   **C** to make

1 I .... be at the party on Saturday.

A don't   **B** not   **C** won't

2 That's my juice. .... is on the table.

A Your   **B** You're   **C** Yours

3 When .... know the answer?

A you will   **B** will   **C** will you

4 You .... drink coffee just before bed.

A should   **B** shouldn't   **C** aren't

5 .... hot and sunny tomorrow.

A It's   **B** It will   **C** It will be

6 You should always .... your teeth after breakfast.

A cleaning   **B** clean   **C** to clean

7 .... is this dictionary?

A Whose   **B** Who's   **C** Who

8 It's ....

A my   **B** mine   **C** your

9 Ben and Jo .... the picnic box.

A will carry   **B** is carrying   **C** carrying

10 Don't eat this cake. It's ....

A there's   **B** theirs   **C** their

4 **Put the words in order.**

be / my / photos / ready / When / will / ?

When will my photos be ready?...............

1 in / the / You / should / sun / sunglasses / wear

....

....

2 money / give / My / parents / some / will / us

....

....

3 chewing gum / drop / in / People / playground / shouldn't / the

....

....

4 any / at / be / my Dad's / good music / party / There won't

....

....

5 and / my / I'm / pen / You're / yours / using / using

....

....

5 **Circle the correct word.**

Take your jacket. It (will / won't) be cold by the lake.

1 You (should / shouldn't) look at the sun. It's (good / bad) for your eyes.

2 (Whose / Who's) are these delicious sweets? Are they (yours / her)?

3 You (should / shouldn't) wear (your / you're) hat in the sun.

4 Where (will / are) you be (at / in) five o'clock?

5 (Their / They're) our CDs, not (there's / theirs).

4 Extra!

1 Where can you see these signs?
Circle A, B or C.

EXAMPLE

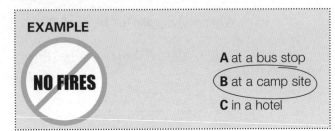

NO FIRES

A at a bus stop
B at a camp site
C in a hotel

1

DO NOT GIVE FOOD
TO THE ANIMALS

A at a beach
B in a market
C at a zoo

2

NO SURFING

A at a beach
B in a café
C at the doctor's

3

TAKE YOUR
LITTER HOME

A in a classroom
B in a café
C at a beach

4

3rd floor:	Café
2nd floor:	Men's clothes
1st floor:	Women's clothes
Ground floor:	Jewellery

A in a supermarket
B in a department store
C in a jeweller's

5

FREE
poster
inside

A on a magazine
B in a school
C in a shop

2 Complete the five dialogues.
Circle A, B or C.

EXAMPLE

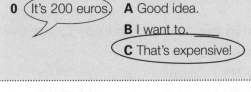

0 It's 200 euros.
A Good idea.
B I want to.
C That's expensive!

1 Stop it!
A Where?
B Yes, please.
C Sorry!

2 Let's go swimming.
A Great idea!
B Hurry up!
C It's lovely.

3 I love those trainers!
A Here we are.
B Me, too!
C Yes, they are.

4 Will you help me?
A Yes, of course.
B Yes, I am.
C Yes, I do.

5 Hurry up!
A When?
B I won't be long.
C That sounds good.

6 Why don't we go to Greenwich?
A I know!
B It's a long way.
C Watch out!

7 It's going to snow.
A No, it isn't.
B I like it.
C What's the weather like?

8 It'll be cold later.
A He's got an umbrella.
B I'll take a jumper.
C We'll find it.

9 Are you doing anything special tomorrow?
A It's my favourite day.
B I like parties.
C No, not really.

10 Let's go to the concert.
A We won't get tickets.
B Here we are.
C I'll just watch.

3 Match the signs (A–H) to the meanings (1–5). There are two extra signs.

EXAMPLE

0 Do not make any noise   [B]

---

1 Come back tomorrow.   [ ]

2 Children don't pay.   [ ]

3 The shop is shut for fourteen days.   [ ]

4 You mustn't drive cars or ride motorcycles here.   [ ]

5 You must bring your own food.   [ ]

A Restaurant closed until 31st January

B SILENCE AT ALL TIMES!

C BICYCLES ONLY

D Closed for two weeks

E DRINKS AND SNACKS ALL DAY

F KIDS GO FREE

G The Office is Closed Today

H Bring a packed lunch

4 Write a letter to your pen-friend inviting him/her to come and stay. Tell him/her your plans for the summer holidays. He/she needs to know the answer to these questions:

- when does your term end?
- how long is your holiday?
- when exactly would you like your pen-friend to visit?

You must also give this information in the letter:

- write about three things you are going to do in the holidays (e.g stay with cousins, play a lot of tennis, visit friends in ….)
- write about some places you will take him/her to visit in your town/area

Write about 120 words, starting and ending like this:

Dear

....

....

....

....

....

....

....

....

....

....

....

....

....

....

....

....

....

....

I hope you can come and stay with me this holiday.

Best wishes ....

GRAMMAR FILE

Comparatives and superlatives

Short adjectives

Adjective	Comparative	Superlative
tall	taller	the tallest
short	shorter	the shortest
nice	nicer	the nicest
large	larger	the largest
hot	hotter	the hottest
big	bigger	the biggest
thin	thinner	the thinnest
dry	drier	the driest

- We form the comparative of short adjectives by adding *er* or *r* to the adjective, e.g. *old/older, late/later.* When the adjective ends in *e*, we add just *r*.
- We form the superlative of short adjectives by putting *the* in front of the adjective and adding *est* or *st* to the end of the adjective, e.g. *old/the oldest, large/the largest.*
- With some short adjectives we double the final consonant in the comparative and superlative, e.g. *big/bigger/the biggest, hot/hotter/the hottest, thin/thinner/the thinnest.*
- With adjectives that end in *y*, we drop the *y* and add *ier* in the comparative and *iest* in the superlative, e.g. *dry/drier/the driest.*

Long adjectives

Adjective	Comparative	Superlative
popular	more popular	the most popular
exciting	more exciting	the most exciting
famous	more famous	the most famous
boring	more boring	the most boring
easy	easier	the easiest
funny	funnier	the funniest

- We form the comparative of some long adjectives by putting *more* in front of the adjective, e.g. *interesting/more interesting, difficult/more difficult.*
- We form the superlative of these long adjectives by putting *the most* in front of the adjective, e.g. *interesting/the most interesting, difficult/the most difficult.*
- With long adjectives that end in *y*, we drop the *y* and add *ier* in the comparative and *iest* in the superlative, e.g. *happy/happier/the happiest, silly/sillier/the silliest.*

Irregular adjectives

Adjective	Comparative	Superlative
good	better	the best
bad	worse	the worst

- *good* and *bad* have irregular comparatives and superlatives.

Sentences with comparative adjectives

Aisha is taller than me.

Maths is more interesting than History.

Sonia is funnier than her brother.

Your bike is better than mine.

Which is worse for you: coffee or cola?

Sentences with superlative adjectives

I'm the youngest in the class.

Venice is one of the most beautiful cities in the world.

I think Geography is the easiest subject.

Who is the best football player in the world?

My mother is the worst singer in our family.

> • We very often use *than* with comparative adjectives, e.g. *My feet are bigger than yours.*

Comparisons with *as ... as ...*

I'm as tall as you now.

Cats are just as clever as dogs.

Volleyball isn't as popular as football.

Is Scotland as cold as Greenland?

Too + adjective

I can't drink this tea. It's too hot.

We can't go swimming today. It's too cold.

Is this room too hot? Would you like me to open a window?

Not + adjective + *enough*

He can't learn to drive yet. He isn't old enough.

We aren't going to the beach today. It isn't warm enough.

I can't put all my things in this bag. It isn't big enough.

> • *too* always comes before the adjective, e.g. *This writing is too small. I can't read it.*
>
> • *Enough* always comes after the adjective, e.g. *We can't eat in the garden today. It isn't warm enough.* NOT: ~~*It isn't enough warm.*~~

5 The highest mountain

Vocabulary

1 Complete the place names on the map using these words.

Sea	Waterfall	Track	Rainforest	Desert	Volcano	South	East
River	Lake	Mountains	Cave	~~Island~~	North	West	

Ithoke ..Island...........................

Nawanga
....

Smokehead
....

The Rainbow
....

The South China
....

The Snowy
....

Pirates
....

Blackwater
....

The Red
....

Calypso's
....

The Cristobal
....

....

....

....

Dialogue work

2 Complete the dialogue with the words below.

- better
- ~~cake~~
- chocolate
- most expensive
- our
- smaller
- spend
- take

Grandmother I'd like a ...cake...., please.

Shop assistant How much do you want to (1) ....?

Grandmother I want the (2) .... one in the shop.

Shop assistant This is (3)..................... biggest cake. It's a coffee cake.

Grandmother Oh dear! My grandson likes (4) .... cakes.

Shop assistant We've got a very nice chocolate cake. It's (5) .... than the coffee cake but it's delicious.

Grandmother Really?

Shop assistant Yes. I think it's (6) .... than the coffee cake. In fact, I think it's the best cake in the shop.

Grandmother Great! I'll (7) .... it.

Grammar practice

3 **Write these sentences with a comparative adjective.**

Portugal / Scotland (cold)

Scotland is colder than Portugal.

1 Egypt / Switzerland (hot)

....

2 Spain / the USA (big)

....

3 July / November (dry) in my country

....

....

4 my hands / my friend's hands (small)

....

....

5 Maths / English (easy)

....

6 films / books (good)

....

7 tennis / football (popular)

....

4 **Write sentences comparing the two girls.**

Zoe	Suzy
1 metre 65	1 metre 63
1 12 years 4 months	1 12 years 6 months
2 very funny !!!!	2 quite funny !!
3 quite patient	3 very patient
4 quite good at music	4 very good at music

Zoe is taller than Suzy.

1 ....

2 ....

3 ....

....

4 ....

....

5 **Write questions with the comparative. Then write answers giving your opinion.**

The Colosseum / the Eiffel Tower (famous)

Which is more famous, the Colosseum or the Eiffel Tower?

Your answer: *The Eiffel Tower* or *The Colosseum*

1 milk / orange juice (expensive)

....

2 birds in cages / hamsters in cages (happy)

....

....

3 tea / coffee (bad for you)

....

....

4 surfing / snowboarding (dangerous)

....

....

5 fruit / chocolate (good for you)

....

....

6 **Use the prompts to make sentences with the superlative. Give your opinion each time.**

beautiful city / Poland

Krakow is the most beautiful city in Poland.

1 bad programme / TV

....

....

2 popular sport / my country

....

....

3 funny person / my class

....

....

4 good singer / my family

....

....

5 hot and dry month / my country

....

....

5

7 **Choose the correct word each time.**

Today is the (longer /(longest) day of the year.

1 My mother makes the (better / best) pancakes.

2 Your dog is (naughtier / naughtiest) than ours.

3 Lucy is the (more popular / most popular) girl in my class.

4 I'm (taller / tallest) than my brother.

5 The Dome Café has the (worse / worst) cakes in this town.

6 Your watch is (more expensive / most expensive) than mine.

7 Are your feet (bigger / biggest) than mine?

8 My mother is (more patient / most patient) than my father.

9 **Write sentences using the prompts.**

do my homework now I / tired
I can't do my homework now. I'm too tired.

1 buy that watch / expensive

....
....

2 wear those jeans / short

....
....

3 wear your shoes / big

....
....

4 do that quiz / difficult

....
....

5 ski down that mountain / dangerous

....
....

8 **Complete the letter with the comparative or superlative of the adjectives in brackets.**

Dear Heidi
I am having one of the ....best........ (good) holidays of my life. We are in Sicily. Sicily is one of the (1)............................. (hot) and (2)............................. (dry) places in Italy, but I love it. Every day we go to the beach. The sea is a lot (3)............................. (warm) than in England. And the ice creams are (4)............................. (good) too.
At the moment we're in Palermo. It's one of the (5).............................. (interesting) towns. There are some beautiful churches and markets here in Sicily. The oranges in Sicily are (6)............................. (big) than the ones in our supermarkets!

Tomorrow we are going to go up Etna. It's a volcano. There are a lot of volcanoes in Italy but Etna is the (7)............................. (big) and the (8)............................. (dangerous). My little brother is a bit frightened about it, but my mother is (9)............................. (frightened) than him! I'm learning some Italian words. I think it's (10).............................. (easy) than Spanish. Ciao for now!
Write to me soon,

Lots of love
Annabel

10 **Complete the sentences with *n't … enough* and the correct adjective. Then match four of the sentences to the pictures.**

deep	hungry	patient	warm
big	~~old~~		tall

We can't see that film.
We .aren't old enough.......................

1 We can't go to the beach today.
It ....

2 I can't open the window.
I ....

3 She won't be a good teacher.
She ....

4 I can't wear your shoes.
They ....

5 We can't eat lunch yet.
We ....

6 Don't jump into the water.
It ....

b

c

a

d

11 **Write sentences with *too* or *not … enough* and the adjective given.**

We aren't going swimming today. (cold)
It's too cold.
....

He won't know the answer. (clever)
He isn't clever enough.
....

1 He doesn't want to go horse riding. (frightened)
....

2 I can't get up yet. (early)
....

3 Her parents never let her go out with her friends. (strict)
....

4 I'm sorry. You can't be in the team yet. (good)
....

5 You can't swim in the sea in February. (warm)
....

6 She can't run in the hundred metre race. (fast)
....

Skills development

Read

1 Read all the information on the page, then answer the questions on the right.

Triangle Films

We are looking for actors for the TV series

Future Stars

Are you between 12 and 15 years old? Can you sing or dance? Can you play the guitar or piano? Are you a good swimmer? Can you ride? Are you good at other sports?

Will you be free for filming in August?

Call Sara Levine on 0208 950 142

Auditions are at Triangle Films, Golden Square on Saturday 7th June at 10 a.m.

7th June Triangle Films: Future Stars

Name:	Mick Porelli
Age:	13 years and 3 months
Height:	1 metre 72
Sports:	Very sporty. 'I love sport. I'm in the school football, tennis and athletics teams. I also swim, ski and snowboard.'
Music:	'I'm OK. I play the guitar but I'm not very good. I'm not a very good singer.
Dancing:	~~OK~~ / (Good) / ~~Excellent.~~ 'I like dancing. I'm doing a dance in our school play.'
Personality:	Very friendly.
Phone number:	020 874 1064

7th June Triangle Films: Future Stars

Name:	Melissa Bradley
Age:	12 years 5 months
Height:	1 metre 60
Sports:	Not very sporty. Can't swim.
Music:	Very musical. Sings and plays the guitar in two bands.
Dancing:	(OK) / ~~Good~~ / ~~Excellent.~~ 'I can dance but I'm not very good.'
Personality:	Good at telling jokes. Quite friendly.
Phone number:	07713 15328

7th June Triangle Films: Future Stars

Name:	Chloe Harris
Age:	12 years 10 months
Height:	1 metre 64
Sports:	Quite sporty. Likes swimming and skating.
Music:	Quite musical. Plays the piano but doesn't sing.
Dancing:	~~OK~~ / ~~Good~~ / (Excellent) Dances rock'n'roll, salsa, tango. 'Dancing is my life.'
Personality:	Very shy.
Phone number:	07815 19805

1 How old must the actors be?

....

2 When will filming begin?

....

3 Who is the youngest?

....

4 Who is the oldest?

....

5 Who is the tallest?

....

6 Who is the shortest?

....

7 Who is the most musical?

....

8 Who's best at sport?

....

9 Who is the best dancer?

....

10 Who is the best singer?

....

11 Who is the funniest?

....

12 Who is the friendliest?

....

Write

2 **Imagine you went to the audition. Complete a form about yourself.**

7th June

Triangle Films: Future Stars

Name: ....

Age: ....

Height: ....

Sports: ....

....

' .... '

Music: ....

....

' .... '

Dancing: OK / Good / Excellent

....

Personality: ....

....

Phone number: ....

Study tips

3 **When you look a word up in the dictionary, it's useful to know if it's a verb or a noun. Write V (verb) or N (noun) for the underlined words.**

My first <u>love</u> is football. [n]

They <u>love</u> athletics. [v]

1 We're going to learn two new <u>dances</u> next week. [   ]

2 She <u>dances</u> a lot. She wants to be a dancer. [   ]

3 I <u>play</u> the guitar and the piano. [   ]

4 Mark was very good in the school <u>play</u>. [   ]

5 Please <u>answer</u> this question. [   ]

6 I'm sorry, I don't know the <u>answer</u>. [   ]

7 Do you want to go for a bike <u>ride</u> tomorrow? [   ]

8 I never <u>ride</u> my bike to school. [   ]

5 Talk time

1 **Write the sentences in the correct balloons.**

- I won't be long.
- No, I'll just watch.
- It's lovely! Jump in!
- We'll meet in the usual place.
- You shouldn't swim straight after lunch.

See you all in Africa.

4 ....

....

1 ....

....

....

3 ....

2 ....

Hurry up!

5 ....

....

2 **Choose the correct response.**

- Hang on a minute!
- I don't know.
- I don't think so.
- I know.
- ~~I think so too.~~

I think everyone needs to do some sport.

I think so too.....................................

1 I'm leaving now. I can't wait for you.

....

2 Who's the most famous British singer?

.... Who is it?

3 *Top of the Pops* is on TV tonight.

.... Let's watch it together.

4 I think Geography is the most boring subject.

.... I really like it.

56

Let's check

1 Choose the correct word for each clue.

cave	lake	rainforest	track
desert	mountains	river	volcano
island	~~north~~	sea	

Bilbao is in the north... of Spain.

1 It's a very hot and dry place. ....

2 There are a lot of trees here. ....

3 It's dark and cold inside it. ....

4 It's a very small road. You can walk on it but it's not for cars. ....

5 There's a fire in this mountain. ....

6 Ireland is one. ....

7 There is usually snow on the highest ones. ....

8 When you go to the beach, you swim in it. ....

9 Baykal is in Russia. ....

10 The Thames is one in England. ....

2 Choose the correct word.

My father is the ..tallest... person in my family.

A taller   B tallest   C the tallest

1 I can't do my Maths homework. It's .... difficult.

A more   B too   C not

2 I prefer you with .... hair.

A longer   B the longer   C the longest

3 Sara is funnier .... her sister.

A for   B of   C than

4 It isn't going to snow. It isn't ....

A cold enough   B colder   C too cold

5 Our town is the .... place in England.

A boring   B more boring   C most boring

3 Put the words in order, to make sentences.

Love / important / is / money / more / than
Love is more important than money.

1 a / because / can't / cold / have / I / is / shower / the / too / water

....
....

2 aren't / because / can't / enough / film / old / see / that / You / you

....
....

3 country / Football / is / more / in my / popular / tennis / than

....
....

4 famous / is / most / one of / singers / the / today / Britney Spears

....
....

4 Fill the gaps with the comparative or superlative of the adjectives.

My school is called Hampton High School. It's ....the biggest. (big) school in the area.

Three people in my class are really good at sport – Martha, Joey and Pete. Pete is the (1)....................... (good) at tennis but Joey is (2)....................... (good) than Pete at swimming. Martha is the (3)............................... (fast) runner in the class. Martha is also the (4)............................... (popular) girl in the class. Everyone likes her. One of the (5)....................................... (interesting) teachers at our school is Mrs Murdoch. She is (6)............................... (patient) than a lot of teachers and she speaks lots of languages. I'm quite a good student. My (7)............................... (bad) subject is Physics. And I think Chemistry is (8)... (difficult) than Biology.

6

GRAMMAR FILE

Verb *to be* Past simple

Affirmative

I was at school yesterday.
You were at school yesterday.
She/He/It was at school yesterday.
We were at school yesterday.
You were at school yesterday.
They were at school yesterday.

- We often use *was/were* with time phrases like *yesterday, last week, last year, two months ago,* e.g. *We were in France last week. It was cold yesterday. There wasn't any hot water this morning.*
- There is no affirmative short form of *was/were.*

Negative

Long form	Short form
I was not at home.	I wasn't at home.
You were not at home.	You weren't at home.
She/He/It was not at home.	She/He/It wasn't at home.
We were not at home.	We weren't at home.
You were not at home.	You weren't at home.
They were not at home.	They weren't at home.

Questions

Was I late yesterday?
Were you late yesterday?
Was she/he/it late yesterday?
Were we late yesterday?
Were you late yesterday?
Were they late yesterday?

- When we make questions with *was/were,* we put the verb before the subject, e.g. *Was she late? Were you out yesterday afternoon? What was the weather like in Scotland?*

Short answers

Affirmative	Negative
Yes, I was.	No, I wasn't.
Yes, you were.	No, you weren't.
Yes, she/he/it was.	No, she/he/it wasn't.
Yes, we were.	No, we weren't.
Yes, you were.	No, you weren't.
Yes, they were.	No, they weren't.

Past simple: regular verbs

Affirmative

I played tennis.
You worked.
She/He/It stayed at home.
We arrived late.
You watched TV.
They visited friends.

Negative

Short form	Long form
I didn't play football.	I did not play football.
You didn't watch TV.	You did not watch TV.
She/He/It didn't visit friends.	She/He/It did not visit friends.
We didn't arrive early.	We did not arrive early.
You didn't work.	You did not work.
They didn't stay at home.	They did not stay at home.

- We use the Past simple for actions that happened at a definite time in the past. We often use it with time expressions like *yesterday, last month, last summer, in July, in 2002*, e.g. *We stayed with our friends in Paris last summer. Alice didn't like the food at the party yesterday. Where did you play tennis?*

- Regular verbs in the Past simple affirmative always end in -ed. But there are spelling rules:
  If the base form ends in e, we add -d, e.g. *like/liked, arrive/arrived, phone/phoned.*
  If the base form ends in a consonant, we add -ed, e.g. *stay/stayed, work/worked, visit/visited.*
  If the base form ends in a consonant + y, we delete the y and add -ied, e.g. *cry/cried, try/tried, carry/carried.*
  With some verbs ending in a consonant, we double the consonant and add -ed, e.g. *stop/stopped, clap/clapped.*

Questions

Did I talk a lot?
Did you enjoy the film?
Did she/he/it work?
Did we watch TV?
Did you play tennis?
Did they walk?

Short answers

Affirmative	Negative
Yes, I did.	No, I didn't.
Yes, you did.	No, you didn't.
Yes, she/he/it did.	No, she/he/it didn't.
Yes, we did.	No, we didn't.
Yes, you did.	No, you didn't.
Yes, they did.	No, they didn't.

- To make a negative statement in the Past simple, we use *didn't* + the base form, e.g. *I didn't stay with my cousins last week. They didn't play cards yesterday.*

- To make a question in the Past simple, we use *did* + the base form, e.g. *Did you watch the match? When did they arrive? Did you enjoy the party?*

6

Where were you last night?

Vocabulary

1 **Match the types of TV programme to the pictures.**

- advert
- cartoon
- comedy programme
- documentary
- music programme
- nature programme
- news
- quiz show
- ~~soap opera~~
- sports programme
- weather

soap opera

Dialogue work

2 **Complete the dialogue with the sentences below.**

- Did you watch *House of Psycho*?
- I'm not telling you. You're still too young for that kind of film!
- ~~Where were you last night?~~
- Why were you frightened?
- You mean Mr Boletus. He was so funny!

Alex Where were you last night?

Kate At Sophie's.

Alex (1) ....

....

Kate We watched a bit. Then we stopped because we were too frightened!

Alex (2) ....

Kate We didn't like that horrible man with the long fingers.

Alex (3) ....

....

Kate What happened at the end?

Alex (4) ....

....

Grammar practice

3 Choose the correct verb.

Jamie (was / were) really annoying on Saturday.

1 You (was / were) brilliant in the match. Well done!

2 I (was / were) really tired after the concert.

3 There (was / were) a storm yesterday when we (was / were) at the beach.

4 My parents (was / were) angry because there (was / were) a mess in the kitchen after our party.

5 Sandra (was / were) happy yesterday because there (was / were) three letters for her.

6 Joey and I (was / were) late this morning because there (was / were) a problem with the buses.

7 My jeans (was / were) on the chair last night but I can't find them today.

8 The match on TV last night (was / were) really boring.

4 Write the sentences in the negative.

1 I was at the party on Friday.

   I wasn't at the party on Friday.

2 It was very cold yesterday.

   ....

3 You were late for school yesterday.

   ....

4 Mum and Dad were strict with my younger sister.

   ....

   ....

5 I was hungry at dinner time.

   ....

6 We were ready for the Maths test.

   ....

   ....

7 Sonia was very lucky in the tennis match.

   ....

   ....

5 Complete the conversation with was(n't) or were(n't).

A: What ..was.. the film like yesterday?

B: It (1) .... brilliant.

A: Who (2) .... in it?

B: There (3) .... an excellent new actor in it called Teresa Paz. She (4) .... really good. Sandra Bullock and Hugh Grant (5) .... also in it.

A: (6) .... Sandra Bullock good?

B: Yes, she (7) .... but she (8) .... as good as Teresa Paz.

A: (9) .... there any dancing in the film?

B: No, there (10) .... But there (11) .... a lot of good music.

A: (12) .... it a comedy?

B: No, it (13) .... but there (14) .... some funny moments in the film.

6 Complete the answers. Then write questions for the answers with What was/were ... like? and the words in the box.

- the match
- the hotel
- the party
- the people
- the play
- the restaurant
- the weather

What was the hotel like?

Beautiful. There .was. (be) a big swimming pool.

1 ....

   Exciting. It .... (be) Porto v Benfica.

2 ....

   Fantastic! It .... (be) really sunny.

3 ....

   The actors .... (be) excellent.

4 ....

   The pizzas .... (not / be) very good.

5 ....

   OK but the music .... (be) a bit boring.

6 ....

   Very kind. Everyone .... (be) really helpful.

7 Write questions and answers with *was* and *were*.

Alex / school / Monday?

No / Paris

Q: Was Alex at school on Sunday?

A: No, he was in Paris.

1 you / at home / last night?

No / Sophie's house

Q: ....

A: ....

2 Mark / in London / yesterday evening?

No / a train to Brighton

Q: ....

....

A: ....

....

3 we / in Greece / August?

No / Spain

Q: ....

A: ....

4 your parents / at work / this morning?

No / the supermarket

Q: ....

....

A: ....

....

5 I / at school / last Monday afternoon?

No / the dentist

Q: ....

....

A: ....

....

8 Write the correct verbs in the gaps in the Past simple.

phone	enjoy	practise	watch
~~be~~	invite	stay	walk
cook	play	stop	

Yesterday the weather ....was....... horrible so we (**1**)........................ at home. First we (**2**)............................ computer games. Then we (**3**) .... our song for the school concert. After that, we (**4**)............................. Pop Machine on TV. At six thirty the rain (**5**)..................... and we (**6**)........................ Jen. She (**7**)........................... us to dinner. So we (**8**)....................... to Jen's house and she (**9**)....................... a delicious meal for us. We (**10**)............................. the evening very much.

9 Write pairs of sentences in the Past simple.

Jane (not clean) the bathroom. I (clean) it.

Jane didn't clean the bathroom.

I cleaned it.

1 We (not work) in a restaurant. We (work) in a café.

....

....

2 Dad (not pick) me up after school. Mum (pick) me up.

....

....

3 I (not start) the fight. He (start) it.

....

....

4 Kate (not like) the video. Sophie (like) it a lot.

....

....

5 Dad (not laugh) at the film. Mum (laugh) a lot.

....

....

6 You (not answer) the phone. Your sister (answer) it.

....

....

10 Complete the questions and answers in the Past simple. Then match the questions and answers.

(Tania / enjoy) her holiday?

Did Tania enjoy her holiday? .... [e]

1 (you play) in the match on Saturday?

....

.... [ ]

2 What time (you start) your sponsored walk?

....

.... [ ]

3 (you / watch) the film?

.... [ ]

4 (you finish) the test?

.... [ ]

a) Yes, but I (not be) very good.

....

b) We (watch) it for ten minutes then the video (stop).

....

....

c) No, I only (answer) two questions. They (be) really difficult.

....

....

d) I'm not sure. But we (finish) at six.

....

e) Yes, she really (like) it a lot.

Yes, she really liked it a lot. ....

11 Look at the calendar and complete the sentences with the time phrases in the box. Write the verbs in the Past simple.

- on Thursday afternoon
- last night
- on Wednesday evening
- the day before yesterday
- this morning
- yesterday lunchtime
- yesterday morning

J U N E	Monday 6	Thursday 9	Sunday 12
	Tuesday 7	Friday 10	
	Wednesday 8	Saturday 11	

I ......stayed.......... (stay) in and ...watched.... (watch) a video .....last night....... . (11th June 9.00 – 11.00 p.m)

1 I .... (play) tennis with Lydia

.... (11th June 10.00 a.m.)

2 I .... (finish) my Science project

.... (9th June 2.00 p.m.)

3 I .... (call) Oliver in New York and

.... (talk) to him for half an hour

.... (8th June 7.00 p.m.)

4 I .... (clean) the car for Dad

.... (12th June 10.00 a.m.)

5 .... (11th June 1.00 p.m.)

I .... (cook) sausages on the barbecue.

6 I .... (cook) dinner for my family ....

.... (10th June)

12 Write short form answers to the questions.

Are you hungry? Yes, ..I am..........................

Does she know him? No, ..she doesn't.......

1 Can he play tennis?

Yes, ...

2 Have you got it?

No, ...

3 Did she tell you?

Yes, ...

4 Do you like chocolate?

Yes, ...

5 Were they annoyed?

No, ...

6 Will it be difficult?

Yes, ...

7 Was it interesting?

No, ...

8 Was there a problem?

Yes, ...

9 Has he got any money?

Yes, ...

10 Can she do it?

No, ...

11 Did they see us?

No, ...

Culture spot

A weekend in Dorset

1 ☐

2 ☐

3 ☐

4 ☐

5 ☐

Friday July 24th

This is Day One of my trip to Dorset with the West London Guides. We travelled from London by **coach**. We stopped at Stonehenge on the way and looked around. It's the oldest 'building' in Britain – it's 5,000 years old. It was a **temple** to the sun **god**.

We arrived at our campsite here in Wareham at four o'clock. In half an hour we're all going to put up our tents. I'm with Lise, Mel and Saskia. The campsite is beautiful. It's in a forest and it's very quiet.

Saturday July 25th

This morning we visited Corfe Castle. It's about a thousand years old and it's just a **ruin** now with no **roof** and a few **walls**. But the **atmosphere** is great. After lunch we're going riding in Wareham Forest. I'm a bit frightened of horses but I'll ask for a nice, slow horse. I only like really quiet old horses!!!

Sunday July 26th

I'm so tired. Today we walked 15 kilometres. We walked from Durdle Door to Tyneham Village and back again. We started with a swim at Durdle Door. Durdle Door is a **rock** in the sea that looks like a door. You can swim through the 'door', but we didn't. I think it's one of the most beautiful beaches in Britain. The water wasn't too cold and it was lovely and **calm**, no wind, or **waves**. Then we started our walk. We walked along the South West Coast Path to Lulworth. It's a really pretty village. We stopped there for an ice cream and a drink. Then we walked to Tyneham Village. It's a very **strange** place, a bit like a museum. One day in 1943 everyone suddenly **abandoned** the village because of the **war**. They never **returned**. We visited the school. All the exercise books and children's drawings were still on the old desks. Nobody uses the school now and nobody lives in the village.

1. Read Jenny's diary and match the captions to the photos.

a) The classroom at Tyneham Village.

b) Durdle Door is a rock with a 'door' in it. You can swim through the door.

c) Lise, Mel, Saskia and I can put a tent up in fifteen minutes!

d) This is Britain's oldest building.

e) Kings and queens don't live in Corfe Castle now.

2. Read Jenny's diary and write short answers to these questions.

1 How old is Stonehenge?

....

2 What's the campsite like?

....

3 How old is Corfe Castle?

....

4 Is Jenny a good rider?

....

5 How many kilometres did the girls walk on Sunday?

....

6 What was the water like at Durdle Door beach?

....

7 Where did the girls stop at a café?

....

8 Who lives in Tyneham Village?

....

3. Guess the meaning of these words and write the translation. Then check in a dictionary.

coach ....

temple...

god ....

ruin ....

roof ....

walls ....

atmosphere..

rock ....

calm ....

waves ....

strange ....

abandon ....

war ....

return ....

Portfolio

4. Tick (✓) the things that are true for you.

Me and nature

I like:

camping	[ ]	going for long walks	[ ]
riding	[ ]	going for long	
swimming in		bike rides	[ ]
the sea	[ ]		
skiing	[ ]		

I can:

read a map	[ ]	use a compass	[ ]
put up a tent	[ ]	cook food outside	[ ]

I'm a bit frightened of:

dogs	[ ]	horses	[ ]	the dark	[ ]
the sea	[ ]	spiders	[ ]	forests	[ ]
snakes	[ ]				

Write about your favourite outdoor activities. Start like this:

My favourite outdoor activity is ....

I usually do it with .... (*name the people you do it with*) in .... (*write the season ot the month*). I like it because

....

I also enjoy ....

I don't like .... (*Name an outdoor activity you don't like*) because ....

....

The thing I'm most frightened of is ....

6

Let's read

Let's stay in the tent

1 **Match the 6 conversations to the pictures. Write the correct number in the boxes.**

1
I'm not going in the water. It's too cold.

Don't be silly. It's lovely and warm.

2
Who wants another sausage?

I do!

3
How do we get to Lulworth Cove?

Let me see the map.

4
There's something wrong with this tent.

You're right. It's going to fall down.

5
I hate this weather.

Let's stay in the tent for a bit.

6
Do you like riding?

It's great but I'm not very good at it.

Let's check

1 **Read the words heard on TV and write the type of programme next to them.**

- advert
- comedy programme
- music programme
- nature programme
- news
- quiz show
- sports programme
- weather

'Do you know the joke about the chicken?! ....'

...comedy programme...

1 'Buy Woof. It's the best dog food.'

....

2 'Tomorrow will be hot and sunny in the south.'

....

3 'This is the most exciting match of the year.'

....

4 'Pink Kisses are the top band this week.'

....

5 'The police say the man is very dangerous.'

....

6 'The giraffes see the lion and start to run.'

....

7 'Now, for ten points, which is the longest river in the world?'

....

2 **Choose the correct word.**

They ...watched.. two videos yesterday evening.

A watching **B** watched **C** watch

1 Where .... you yesterday afternoon?

A were **B** was **C** did

2 Who .... the dinner last Sunday?

A cooks **B** did cook **C** cooked

3 My sister .... enjoy her holiday last summer.

A doesn't **B** wasn't **C** didn't

4 There .... any nice trainers in the shop.

A weren't **B** were **C** wasn't

5 When .... finish her English project?

A she did **B** did she **C** was she

6 There .... any milk in the fridge.

A weren't **B** wasn't **C** was

7 'Did you stay with your cousins?' 'Yes, we ....'

A did **B** stayed **C** were

8 We played computer games ....

A after dinner **B** tomorrow **C** now

9 'Did they like the film?' 'No, they ....'

A didn't like **B** weren't **C** didn't

10 Who .... at the party on Saturday?

A were **B** was **C** did

3 **Write the verbs in the Past simple.**

Hi Erica

I really (**1**)...liked.......... (like) your last e-mail and I'm sorry I (**2**)............................... (not answer) it before.

In July I (**3**) .... (work) in a café for two weeks and (**4**) .... (save) some money.

Then my friend Katerina (**5**) .... (invite) me to Greece. I (**6**) .... (stay) with her for three weeks. We (**7**) .... (visit) a beautiful island called Sifnos. One day we (**8**) .... (walk) about 15 kilometres to a beautiful beach. We (**9**) .... (be) really hot so we (**10**) .... (stop) at a café. In the café I (**11**) .... (play) a game called tavoli with a very old Greek man.

(**12**) .... (you stay) in London this summer? (**13**) .... (it rain) every day? How (**14**) .... (be) your exams? Mine (**15**) .... (not / be) too bad. Write soon.

Love Holly

Reading comprehension

 Read the text and answer the questions.

The Simpsons **are the most popular family in the world. Every week, millions of people all over the world stay at home to watch them on TV. This cartoon family of five people all have ugly yellow faces, big white eyes and strange hairstyles.**

The parents are Homer and Marge. Homer works in a nuclear power plant and spends all his free time watching TV and eating doughnuts. He always eats with his mouth open and he's too fat. Marge has blue hair. She loves her tall hairstyle and goes to the hairdresser's twice a day. She's always very kind to her family. Bart is the oldest child. He is very naughty at school and always gets bad marks. He doesn't do his homework and he's often rude to his parents. His favourite answer to his father is 'Eat my shorts, (Pa).' He likes skateboarding and playing tricks on his sister, Lisa. Lisa is a bit younger than Bart and is always top of the class at school. She's the cleverest person in the family. She's a very good saxophone player. Maggie is the youngest child. She can't talk or walk but she's always in a good mood. She can only say one word – *Daddy*.

The Simpsons started in 1990 and it's still very popular. People of all ages like it because *The Simpsons* are like a real family. They aren't perfect and beautiful like a lot of families on TV.

1 What kind of programme is *The Simpsons*?

....

2 What do the Simpsons look like?

....

....

3 What colour is Marge's hair?

....

4 Who's the oldest child in the family?

....

5 What is Bart like at school?

....

....

6 Who is the cleverest person in the family?

....

7 Which musical instrument does Lisa play?

....

8 Which word can Maggie say?

....

9 When did the programme start?

....

10 Why is it so popular?

....

....

11 How much TV do you watch every day?

....

....

12 What's your favourite kind of TV programme and why?

....

....

2 Complete the dialogue. What does Josie say to Adam? Choose from A–H. There are two extra responses.

> EXAMPLE
>
> **Adam** Are you doing anything special tomorrow?
>
> **Josie** 0 ...C........

Adam Would you like to come to the beach with us?

Josie 1 ....

Adam Joey and I will make some sandwiches.

Josie 2 ....

Adam Great! Where's the best place to meet?

Josie 3 ....

Adam Fine.

Josie 4 ....

Adam There's a bus to Linton Beach at eleven thirty.

Josie 5 ....

Adam Because I never get up before ten on Sundays.

Josie OK. I'll see you both there at eleven fifteen then.

A How about at the bus station?
B Yes, I like that very much.
C No, I'm not.
D OK. I'll bring some drinks.
E This picnic is great.
F What time should I be there?
G Why don't we get the earlier one?
H Yes, I'd love to.

3 Read this note from your friend, Emma.

> Have a great holiday!
> Don't forget to send me a postcard. I want to know where you are, who you're with and what you do every day.
> I also want to know about the hotel, the food and the weather.
> Emma

Write Emma a postcard. Answer her questions about your holiday.
Write 30–40 words.

7

GRAMMAR FILE

Expressions of quantity

	Affirmative sentences	Negative sentences	Questions
Plural countable nouns	a lot of lots of plenty of a few	many	many
Uncountable nouns	a lot of lots of plenty of a little	much	much

Plural countable nouns

Affirmative sentences
There are a lot of new students in my class this year.
I've got lots of friends at my school.
There are plenty of pencils in the drawer.
I talked to a few people at Sandy's party.

Negative sentences
There weren't many people at the beach yesterday.
I don't buy many new CDs.

Questions
Do you know many English songs?
How many questions did you answer in the test?

Uncountable nouns

Affirmative sentences
There's a lot of money in this bag.
Adam likes lots of milk on his cereal.
There's plenty of juice in the fridge.
I like my coffee with a little sugar.

Negative sentences
Hurry up. We haven't got much time.
I don't spend much money on magazines.

Questions
Does your hamster drink much water?
How much money are you taking with you?

- We can use *a lot of, lots of* and *plenty of* with countable and uncountable nouns. *I've got a lot of new CDs. There's a lot of milk in the fridge. We played lots of games. There's lots of juice on the table. There are plenty of apples in the bag. There's plenty of fruit in the kitchen.*

- We use *a few* with countable nouns and *a little* with uncountable nouns, e.g. *There are a few lemons in the fridge. Can I have a little milk in my tea, please?*

- We often use the words *just* or *only* with *a few* and *a little*, e.g. *There are just a few sweets left. I want just a little cheese on my spaghetti, please.*

- We use *many* with countable nouns and *much* with uncountable nouns, e.g. *She didn't ask many questions. Hurry! We haven't got much time.*

Past simple: irregular verbs

Affirmative

I went home early yesterday.
You made pancakes yesterday.
She/He/It had a bath yesterday.
We saw a good film yesterday.
You gave Joey a present yesterday.
They came to dinner yesterday.

Negative

I didn't go to bed late yesterday.
You didn't make pizza yesterday.
She/He/It didn't have lunch yesterday.
We didn't see the match yesterday.
You didn't give me a present yesterday.
They didn't come to dinner on Sunday.

Questions

Did I see you yesterday?
Did you come to my party yesterday?
Did she/he/it have breakfast yesterday?
Did we go to the cinema yesterday?
Did you make a cake yesterday?
Did they give you the letters?

Short answers

Affirmative	Negative
Yes, I did.	No, I didn't.
Yes, you did.	No, you didn't.
Yes, she/he/it did.	No, she/he/it didn't.
Yes, we did.	No, we didn't.
Yes, you did.	No, you didn't.
Yes, they did.	No, they didn't.

- A lot of very common verbs have an irregular affirmative form in the Past simple. There are no rules for how to form them. You just have to learn them by heart! There's a list of irregular verbs on page 135 of the Student's Book.
- With irregular verbs in the past simple, we form questions and negatives with *did / didn't* + the base form just as with regular verbs, e.g. *Did you see the match? Where did you go on Saturday? I didn't go out.* We don't say: ~~Did you saw the match? Where did you went on Saturday? I didn't went out.~~

The irregular verbs that you meet in this unit are:

Infinitive	Past simple
be	was
come	came
do	did
eat	ate
fall	fell
get	got
give	gave
go	went
have	had
hit	hit
make	made
put	put
see	saw
send	sent
take	took
throw	threw

7

We made lots of pancakes!

Vocabulary

1 Complete the crossword. All the answers are food words.

Across

1 You need it to make bread.
5 It's white and you drink it.
8 You need them to make chips.
9 You put it on bread or toast.
11 They eat a lot of it in China and India.
12 You put the juice on pancakes.
13 Rabbits like these orange vegetables.

Down

2 You put this on salad with vinegar.
3 Onions, beans and peas are all __.
4 It's always on the table with the salt.
5 Lamb and beef are __.
6 A lot of people eat it for breakfast.
7 They are very small fish.
10 English people love this hot drink.

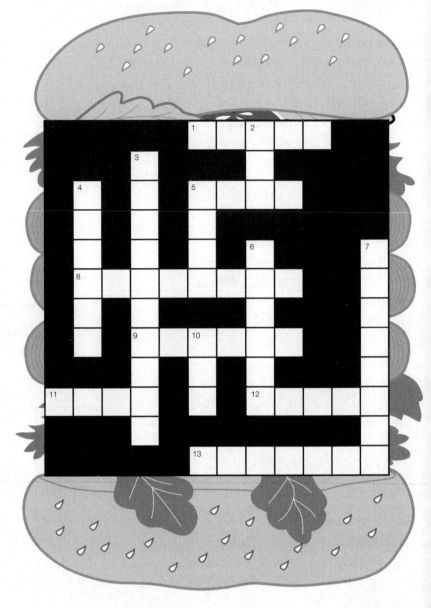

Dialogue work

2 Complete the dialogue with the words in the box.

doing	here's	minute	~~put~~	them
grapes	lots	olives	some	tomato

Sophie What can I ...put.... on this pizza base?

Jamie You need (1) .... sauce and
(2) .... of cheese.

Sophie There's (3) .... tomato sauce in the
fridge. Can you get it, please?

Jamie Here you are. And (4) .... some
mozzarella cheese.

Sophie Let's put some (5) .... on top.

Jamie I don't like olives.

Sophie OK. I'll just put (6) .... on my half.

Jamie Wait a (7) ....

Sophie What are you (8) .... now, Jamie?
Why are you putting olives on your half?

Jamie These aren't olives. They're (9) ....

Grammar practice

3 Write sentences with *a few* or *a little*.

Grandma's Great Big Cheese Cake

~~butter~~   4 flour
~~apples~~   5 grapes
1 bananas   6 lemons
2 cream cheese   7 milk
3 eggs   8 sugar

We need: a little butter   a few apples

1 ....   5 ....

2 ....   6 ....

   ....   7 ....

3 ....   8 ....

4 ....

4 Complete the sentences with *much* or *many*. Then match the pictures to them.

1 We don't need ..much.. water to have fun. [e]

2 I don't eat .... salad. I prefer strawberries. [ ]

3 I'm sorry, there aren't .... sardines. [ ]

4 Really Mum, I didn't eat .... carrots. [ ]

5 There aren't .... nice apples left. [ ]

6 You can't have .... cheese.
It isn't good for you. [ ]

5 Choose the correct words.

We didn't get (much / plenty of) homework today.

1 There's (plenty of / much) milk in the fridge.

2 We haven't got (much / many) games on our computer.

3 Can I have (a few / a little) mushrooms on my pizza?

4 We've got (lots of / much) news to tell you.

5 There weren't (much / many) people at the swimming pool today.

6 I didn't put (much / plenty of) pepper on your chicken sandwich.

7 Do you want (a few / a little) lemon juice on your pancake?

8 I don't want (much / many) cheese on my pasta, thanks.

9 I didn't buy (plenty of / many) apples.

10 Would you like (a few / a little) sweets to take on the trip?

11 I want (plenty of / much) cheese on my pizza.

12 I don't eat (much / plenty of) meat.

13 We didn't eat (plenty of / many) grapes.

14 There are only (a little / a few) oranges left.

6 **Fill the gaps with the correct verb in the Past simple.**

come	eat	give	have
~~be~~	get	go	make

On Sunday it ...**was**......... my birthday. In the morning,

my sister Alice (**1**) ….......... a chocolate cake for me.

In the evening, I (**2**) …........… a party on the beach.

All my friends (**3**) ….......…. to the party. Serena

(**4**) ….......… me a really nice green T-shirt. First we

(**5**) ….......… swimming. Then we (**6**) …......………

warm by the fire and (**7**) ….......…. some sausages.

7 **Write the questions and answers in the Past simple. Match the questions and answers.**

What (you do) in Scotland?

What did you do in Scotland?......... [e]

1 (you drop) those sweets on the floor?

....

.... [ ]

2 (you see) Gary in the park?

....

.... [ ]

3 What (you buy) in Paris?

....

.... [ ]

4 Who (throw) this ball into the bathroom?

....

.... [ ]

5 What (you do) last night?

....

.... [ ]

Answers

a) I (spend) all my money on clothes.

....

....

b) No, they (fall) out of my bag, I think.

....

....

c) No. But I (see) his brother.

....

d) I (have) a shower, then I (do) my homework.

....

....

e) We (go) for long walks in the mountains.

We went for long walks in the mountains.

f) I did. But I (not do) it on purpose.

....

....

8 **Write the sentence beginning in the Past simple. Then choose the correct sentence ending.**

1 Anna (draw)

Anna drew a snake on her hand.......... [b]

2 Who (drink) all

....

.... [ ]

3 I (find)

....

.... [ ]

4 My sister (go)

....

.... [ ]

5 My brother (read)

....

.... [ ]

6 We (run) to school today

....

.... [ ]

7 They (speak)

....

.... [ ]

8 Who (take) my diary

....

.... [ ]

a) some money in the street.
b) ~~a snake on her hand.~~
c) because we were late.
d) to New York this morning.
e) from my bag?
f) on the phone for an hour.
g) the orange juice?
h) two books yesterday.

9 **Read Claudia's diary. Put the verbs in the Past simple and number the sentences in the correct order.**

[ ] After that I .... (not have) any money left.

[ ] I .... (feel) really hungry so I .... (have) a big breakfast – cereal, eggs, toast and juice.

[ ] I .... (take) the number 27 bus to Portobello Market and .... (meet) Maria there.

[1] I ....got...... (get) up quite late – about ten o'clock.

[ ] Maria .... (give) me a pound for the bus home.

[ ] They .... (cost) ten pounds.

[ ] We .... (go) into lots of shops. I .... (buy) some earrings for my Mum's birthday.

10 **Put the verbs in the Past simple tense.**

New ▼ | Send | Receive | Forward | Delete

Hello Alex

We .....left...... (leave) London last night. We (**1**) .... (get) to Boston at 11 o'clock this morning.

I (**2**) .... (not sleep) on the plane and I (**3**) .... (not eat) the meal.

Joey and his sister Alice (**4**) .... (meet) us at the airport. Alice (**5**) .... (drive) us

to their house. We all (**6**) .... (be) really hungry. Mrs Coles (**7**) .... (make) us

pasta and a delicious green salad for lunch. We (**8**) .... (have) pancakes and ice cream for

pudding. After lunch I (**9**) .... (feel) very tired so I (**10**) .... (sleep) for half an

hour. After that we (**11**) .... (go) shopping at Quincy Market.

I (**12**) .... (buy) a baseball cap. Joey and Alice (**13**) .... (not buy) anything.

America is amazing! How long (**14**) .... (you stay) in Portugal?

(**15**) .... (you have) a good time? Write soon, Frankie

11 **Write pairs of sentences in the Past simple.**

He (not buy) a CD at the weekend. He (buy) a book.

He didn't buy a CD at the weekend.

He bought a book.

1 Lucy (not forget) her homework yesterday. She (forget) her keys.

....

....

2 My parents (not drive) to Spain last summer. They (drive) to France.

....

....

....

3 I (not wear) jeans to the party on Saturday. I (wear) my new skirt.

....

....

4 Josh (not ride) his bike to school yesterday. He (ride) it to Dan's house.

....

....

5 We (not sit) at the back of the class. We (sit) at the front.

....

....

Skills development

Read

HALLOWE'EN IS FUN

Alice, Jessica, Luke and Dan talk about their favourite day of the year.

'Lots of families buy a **pumpkin** for Hallowe'en. You cut a face in it. It can be happy, sad, funny or frightening. Then you put a candle in your pumpkin, turn all the lights out and put the pumpkin in the window.'

Jessica

'Hallowe'en is on the 31st October. Children wear **masks** and dress up as **ghosts, devils, vampires, skeletons** and **witches**. Then they go trick-or-treating. That means they go to people's houses and say 'trick or treat?' Most people give them a treat – sweets or chocolate perhaps. Some people don't give them anything. Then the children play a trick on them. For example, they throw water at them.'

Alice

'Why do we celebrate Hallowe'en? It's an old tradition, probably more than 2,000 years old. People believed in ghosts and wanted to frighten them away. So they dressed up as ghosts and witches themselves.'

Luke

'Yesterday was Hallowe'en. My friend Ben had a Hallowe'en party. My sister Amy dressed up as a witch. She had a big black hat and a horrible mask. I dressed up as a ghost. My mother gave me an old **sheet** and I used that. It was very difficult to walk and even more difficult to eat! In fact, after about an hour, I took my costume off. At the party we bobbed for apples. It's a special Hallowe'en game. There are apples in a bowl of water and you try to get them out with your mouth. Everybody gets very wet!' Dan

1 **Read the text and match these words to the pictures.**

| ghost | devil | vampire | mask | skeleton | witch | pumpkin | sheet |

1................................... 2................................... 3................................... 4...................................

5................................... 6................................... 7................................... 8...................................

2 **Read the text and circle the correct answer.**

1 Hallowe'en is on:

   A 1st November
   B 2nd November
   C 31st October

2 On Hallowe'en children wear:

   A their best clothes
   B school uniform
   C witch, ghost and vampire costumes

3 Trick-or-treating is:

   A a game with apples
   B making a lamp with a vegetable
   C asking neighbours for sweets

4 A treat can be:

   A a book or magazine
   B sweets or chocolate
   C a glass of water

5 When you bob for apples, you use:

   A your mouth
   B your hands
   C your feet

3 **Write**

Write a letter to a friend about a party. Answer some of these questions in the letter.

- Whose party was it?
- What kind of party was it?
- Did you wear costumes?
- What was the food like?
- What was the music like?
- What did you do at the party?
- When did it start?
- When did it end?
- Did you enjoy it?

Write the letter in your notebook. Start like this:

Dear ....

I went to a party last ....

Study tips

4 **A word web is a good way of learning and remembering new words. Complete this word web.**

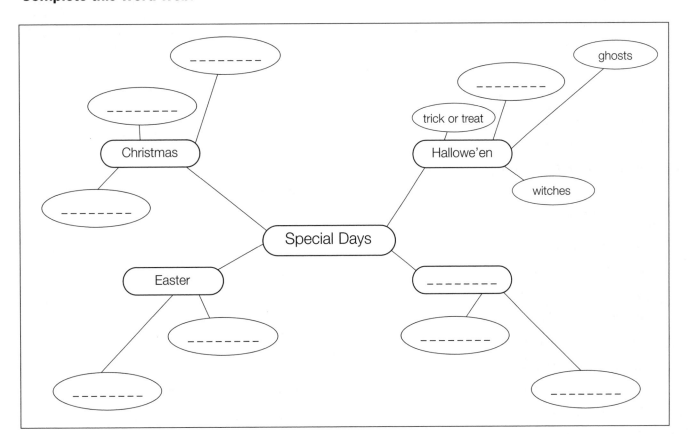

1 Match the sentences to the correct responses.

2 Complete the dialogue with the phrases.

Was your Mum angry about the mess?	[b]
1 Are you doing anything this weekend?	[ ]
2 Let's go for a picnic in Epping Forest.	[ ]
3 What's that book about?	[ ]
4 I was late for school yesterday.	[ ]
5 When is Sport Stars on?	[ ]
6 Will you be out for long?	[ ]
7 You did that on purpose.	[ ]
8 Ooops! Sorry!	[ ]

a) It's about two girls in the circus.

b) ~~Well, she wasn't happy!~~

c) It's on tomorrow at seven.

d) No, I didn't. I'm really sorry.

e) Did you get into trouble?

f) No, why don't you come round?

g) Only for about ten minutes.

h) Oh no! It's all over the floor.

i) Sounds great!

• got into a lot of trouble.	• wasn't happy
• just then	• go all over
• ~~do it on purpose~~	

Chloe I dropped a glass of lemonade on my brother's desk.

Jessica Did you (**1**) ....do it on purpose.........?

Chloe Of course, I didn't.

Jessica Did it (**2**) .... his computer?

Chloe Yes. Anyway, I started to clean it up. But (**3**) .... Liam came in.

Jessica Was he angry?

Chloe Well, he (**4**) .... !

Jessica Did he tell your parents?

Chloe Yes, and I (**5**) ....

Let's check

1 **a) Put the letters in order, to make food and drink words.**
b) Choose the correct title for each group of words.

tutreb	shecee	crame	
butter.......	cheese......	cream........	made.from.milk.
1 inoon	torrac	toopat	
....	....	....	....
2 ate	klim	focefe	
....	....	....	....
3 feeb	malb	mah	
....	....	....	....
4 snabaan	spear	plesap	
....	....	....	....

drinks
~~made from milk~~
fruit
vegetables
meat

2 **Choose the correct word.**

Hurry! We haven't got ...**much**.. time.

A many   **B** much   **C** a lot

1 I'm going to make a .... sandwiches.

     A few   **B** little   **C** lot

2 'Were you late for school?' 'No, we ....'

     A didn't   **B** wasn't   **C** weren't

3 There isn't .... of water in the swimming pool.

     A a lot   **B** plenty   **C** much

4 'Was it hot in Sicily?' 'Yes, it ....'

     A did   **B** was   **C** had

5 There aren't .... American teachers at my school.

     A many   **B** much   **C** a lot

6 'Did she see you?' 'No, she ....'

     A wasn't   **B** saw   **C** didn't

7 We need a .... salt on this chicken.

     A few   **B** little   **C** lot

8 What .... for dinner yesterday?

     A were you   **B** did you   **C** did you have

9 She's got .... of sweets.

     A many   **B** lot   **C** plenty

10 I didn't .... your last e-mail.

     A got   **B** getting   **C** get

3 **Write the verbs in the Past simple.**

Yesterday it ...**was**...... (be) really sunny. I
(1) .... (get) up quite early. My mother
(2) .... (give) me some money and
I **(3)** .... (go) shopping for food for our
picnic. I **(4)** .... (buy) bread, cheese, ham,
fruit and drinks. I **(5)** .... (come) home with
all the food and we **(6)** .... (make)
sandwiches. Then my mum, Flora, Kathy and I
(7) .... (ride) to the beach on our bikes. My
dad **(8)** .... (drive) to the beach with his
friend Sam.

We **(9)** .... (spend) all day at the beach.
I **(10)** .... (swim) and Flora and
Mum **(11)** .... (run) along the sand.
They both **(12)** .... (fall) over but they
(13) .... (be) OK. We all **(14)** ....
(have) a brilliant time. Mum **(15)** .... (wear)
her new sun hat and sunglasses and Dad
(16) .... (take) lots of photos of her.
James **(17)** .... (find) £2 in the sand, lucky
thing. I **(18)** .... (see) some friends from school
and **(19)** .... (say) hello to them. We
(20) .... (leave) the beach at five o'clock.

GRAMMAR FILE

Prepositions of motion

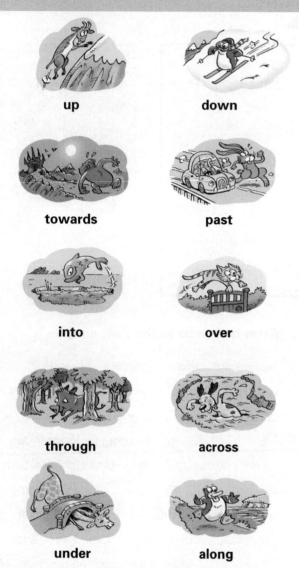

up

down

towards

past

into

over

through

across

under

along

- We use prepositions of motion with verbs like *climb, come, get, go, jump, ride, run, swim, walk.*

We were very tired so we walked **up** the mountain very slowly.

Let's ride **down** the mountain on our bikes.

It started to rain so we all ran **into** the house.

The gate was shut so we climbed **over** the wall.

You can swim **under** the waterfall.

Go **towards** the station and take the first left.

I always run **past** that house because I'm frightened of the dog.

Don't walk **through** the forest. There are dangerous animals in there!

My mother often swims **across** this river. It isn't dangerous.

It's a beautiful day. Let's walk **along** the river.

- You can use the same preposition with a variety of verbs, e.g. *come along, go along, ride along, run along, walk along.*

Time expressions: *ago, last*

ago
I took this photo two years ago. You were ten then.
Is Andy here? No, he left ten minutes ago.
I made coffee an hour ago. It's cold now.
How long ago did you buy this CD?

- We use *ago* + period of time with the Past simple. It means before now, e.g. *three weeks ago* (= three weeks before now), *two days ago* (= two days before now), *ten minutes ago* (=ten minutes before now).

- You can't use *before* instead of *ago*, You must say: *We went there two months ago* NOT ~~We went there two months before.~~

last
When did you last see Julie?
I last saw her in July.
When did you last go to the beach?
I last went to the beach three months ago.

- We use *last* with the Past simple, e.g. *The dog is really dirty. He last had a bath six months ago.*

could for requests

Could you pass me the sugar, please?
Could you help me with my Maths homework?
Could I shut the window, please?
Please could I borrow your ruler for a moment?
Could we come to the beach with you?
Could we leave our bags here?

- We use *could* to make polite requests. It is most common in the first and second persons, *I, we, you*, e.g. *Could you tell me the way to the station? Could I borrow your pen, please?*
- We use *can* or *could* to make requests but *could* is more polite than *can*.
- The usual answers to polite requests with *can* and *could* are *Yes, of course. No, I'm sorry I can't. I'm afraid, I can't*, e.g. *Could you help me with my homework? Yes, of course.* OR: *No, I'm sorry. I can't.*

Imperatives

Affirmative
Walk towards the river.
Negative
Don't go over the bridge.

- We use the imperative to give orders, e.g. *Be quiet. Don't talk.* We also use it to give directions, e.g. *Walk past the station. Don't turn right.*
- To form the affirmative imperative, we use the base form of the verb. To form the negative, we use *don't* + the base form. It's the same in the singular and the plural.
- To make orders in the imperative more polite, we add *please*, e.g. *Please be quiet. Don't talk, please.*

That was 500 years ago!

Vocabulary

along	past
down	~~through~~
into	towards
over	under
over	up

1 Complete each sentence with the correct proposition.

Go .....**through**....... the gate.

1 Walk .... the river.

2 You will come to a bridge. Go .... the bridge.

3 Walk .... the mountain.

4 On the mountain there is a very old house. Walk .... the house.

5 There's a horrible dog near the house. Run .... the dog.

6 You'll see a little path. Go .... the path.

7 Walk .... the big bridge.

8 Go .... the cave and get the box.

9 Climb .... the gate and run back to the town. Do not drop the box.

Dialogue work

2 **Complete the dialogue with the sentences below.**

Kate Where did you go for your summer holidays?

....

Alex We went to Greece.

Kate (1) ....

Alex Yes. It was called Samos.

Kate (2) ....

Alex I went swimming and ate lots of ice cream.

Kate (3) ....

Alex In a pretty white house near the sea.

Kate (4) ....

Alex Yes, a few words. I can say ice cream in Greek, for example!

Kate (5) ....

Alex Yes, I loved it. I want to go back some time.

```
• Did you learn any Greek?
• Did you like Greece?
• Were you on an island?
• What did you do every day?
• Where did you go for your summer holidays?
• Where did you stay?
```

Grammar practice

3 **Write answers in the Past simple with**
days/weeks/hours/months/years + ago.

Remember: we can't say *one day ago*.)

When did you last see a really good film?

I saw a really good film two/three/five days ago.

1 When did you last eat a pizza?

....

....

2 When did you last go swimming?

....

....

3 When did you last buy chewing gum?

....

....

4 When did you last get really angry?

....

....

4 **Write the verbs in the Past simple. Then say how long ago it happened.**

Hannibal ..brought.....(bring) elephants across the Alps in 217 BC. That was about 2,220 .....years ago...

1 Leonardo da Vinci .... (paint) the Mona Lisa in 1503. That was ....

2 Marconi .... (make) the first radio in 1895. That was ....

3 Christopher Columbus ....(sail) to America in 1492. That was ....

4 Giuseppe Verdi .... (write) *Rigoletto* in 1851. That was ....

5 The *Titanic* ....(sink) in 1912. That was ....

6 The Romans .... (arrive) in Britain in 43. That was ....

5 **Choose the correct form of the verb.**

Always (walk / don't walk) across the road carefully.

1 (Speak / Don't speak) Portuguese. This is an English lesson.

2 Here are my letters. Please (post / don't post) them for me at the post office.

3 (Swim / Don't swim) after a big meal. It's dangerous.

4 (Draw / Don't draw) on the desks. It's horrible.

5 Please (be / don't be) quiet. I'm trying to sleep.

6 (Forget / Don't forget) your keys and purse.

7 (Wear / Don't wear) that big sweater tonight. You'll be too hot.

6 **Match the directions to the maps. Write the correct number next to each map.**

1 ~~Go straight on. Take the second turning on the left.~~

2 Turn right at the roundabout. That's Market Street. Then turn right again.

3 Go over the bridge. Take the second turning on the right.

4 Turn left into Market Street. Turn right at the roundabout. Then turn left.

5 Turn right. Go over the bridge. Take the second turning on the left.

6 Go straight on at the roundabout. Go over the bridge and turn right.

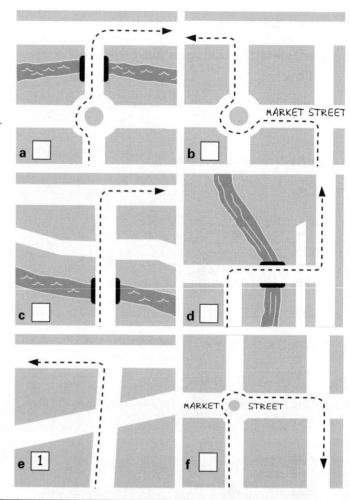

a ☐   b ☐

MARKET STREET

c ☐   d ☐

MARKET STREET

e ☐1   f ☐

7 **Write directions for each map.**

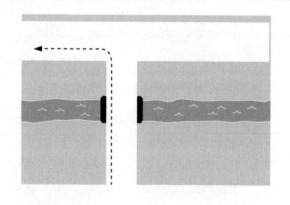

Go over the bridge and turn left.

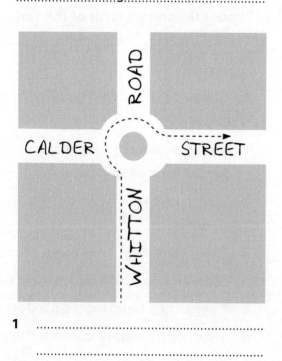

ROAD

CALDER   STREET

WHITTON

1 ....

....

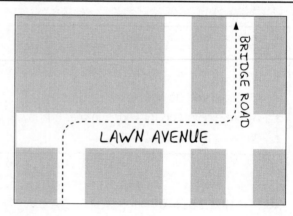

BRIDGE ROAD

LAWN AVENUE

2 ....

....

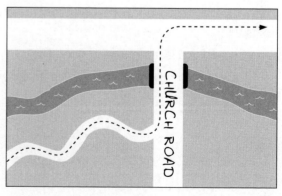

CHURCH ROAD

3 ....

....

8 Match the questions to the pictures. Write the correct number in box.

1 Could I see your tickets, please? 4 Could I have a glass of water, please?
2 ~~Could you take a photo of us, please?~~ 5 Could you carry something, please?
3 Could you pass me a paint brush, please? 6 Could I borrow your comb, please?

a 2

Could you take a photo of us, please?

b ☐

f ☐

c ☐ d ☐

e ☐

9 Write requests with *could I/you*. Then match the requests to the reasons.

borrow your newspaper?

Could I borrow your newspaper? .... [b]

1 buy me some new trainers?

.... [ ]

2 get us some milk and flour?

.... [ ]

3 have your e-mail address?

.... [ ]

4 say that again, please?

.... [ ]

5 speak to Christina?

.... [ ]

6 tell me the time, please?

.... [ ]

7 use your calculator?

.... [ ]

a) I need it for my Maths homework.
b) ~~I want to see the film times.~~
c) I'll send you an invitation to my party.
d) I'm calling about her piano lesson.
e) I'm not wearing my watch today.
f) My English isn't very good yet.
g) These are too small now.
h) We want to make pancakes.

Culture spot
The Tower of London

The Tower of London is Britain's most popular monument. Millions of tourists visit this castle every year. It took 20 years to **build**. William the Conqueror started it in 1078 and finished it in 1098. ▶

▲ You can see royal **crowns** and thousands of **diamonds** in the Tower. They're called the Crown Jewels. One of the diamonds is called the Star of Africa. It's one of the biggest in the world.

◀ For years the Tower was a **prison**. Soldiers brought **prisoners** to the Tower by **boat**. The prisoners came along the river and entered the tower through Traitor's Gate.

In 1483 twelve-year-old Edward became king of England. His uncle, Richard, wanted to be king so he put Edward and his younger brother in the Tower. Nobody saw them again. They both **died** and their horrible uncle became King Richard III. About 200 years later some **workmen** found the boys' skeletons in the Tower.

▼

About 50 years later, Henry VIII put Anne Boleyn and Catherine Howard, two of his six wives, in prison in the Tower. Henry was angry with them because they didn't give him any sons! On Tower Green, Henry's **soldiers cut** Anne's and Catherine's heads off.

◀ Soldiers called Beefeaters work in the Tower now. They show tourists the Tower. And they look after the Crown jewels and the **ravens**, the famous black birds in the gardens of the Tower.

1 Read the text and match these words to the pictures.

raven	soldier	boat	crown
prison	workmen	prisoners	diamond

1. ....

2. ....

3. ....

4. ....

5. ....

6. ....

7. ....

8. ....

2 Guess the meaning of these verbs, then check in your dictionary.

build	die	cut

3 Write T (true) or F (false).

1 A lot of tourists visit The Tower of London. [ ]
2 It's a modern building. [ ]
3 It's a long way from the river. [ ]
4 Richard III was a very kind man. [ ]
5 Workmen found skeletons in the Tower 200 years ago. [ ]
6 Henry VIII married many times. [ ]
7 Two of his wives were in prison in the Tower. [ ]
8 You can see lots of jewels in the Tower. [ ]
9 A raven is a type of jewel. [ ]

Portfolio

4 **Write about you and learning history. Circle the best answers for you, tick (✓) the boxes and write your own words in the space.**

Sightseeing is a *good* / *bad* way of learning history.

I *often* / *sometimes* / *never* visit historic places.

The last historic monument I visited was
....

The most popular historic monument in my country is ....

On our last school trip we went to
....

My favourite period in history is
....

In history I like learning about:
- buildings [ ]
- wars [ ]
- politics [ ]
- kings and queens [ ]
- everyday life (houses, clothes, schools) [ ]

I *often* / *sometimes* / *never* watch history programmes on TV.

The last history programme I saw on TV was about ....

8

Let's read

You can get there by boat

1 **Read Jessy and Emma's conversation and the summary below. Fill each gap in the summary with one word instead of the phrases 1 to 6 in the conversation.**

Conversation

Emma: Hi Jessy. What are you doing today?

Jessy: I want to take my Australian friend Laura to some tourist spots in London.

Emma: Where are you going to take her?

Jessy: I'm not sure. Yesterday we went to Portobello market.

Emma: Did she like it?

Jessy: She loved it. She bought **(1)** **a necklace and earrings.** I bought **(2)** **two T-shirts and a dress.**

Emma: What are you going to do today?

Jessy: I don't know. Have you got any ideas?

Emma: Why don't you go on a boat **(3)** **down the river?** You can get out at the Tower of London. It's really fun **(4)** **on a sunny day.**

Jessy: That's a great idea. Why don't you come with us? We can go **(5)** **after lunch.**

Emma: Why after lunch? What are you doing this morning?

Jessy: Laura wants to buy new shoes.

Emma: There's a good shoe shop in Church Road called Sports Plus. It's got hundreds of shoes. And they **(6)** **don't cost very much.**

Summary

Jessy is taking Laura sightseeing in London today. Yesterday at Portobello Laura bought (1)................ and Jessy bought (2).................... . Emma says a boat (3).................... is fun when the (4).................... is good. They decide to go in the (5) .... Emma says the shoes in Sports Plus aren't (6)..................

---

2 **Read the rest of the conversation and mark the route on the map. Mark the shop with an X.**

Jessy: But where is Sports Plus?

Emma: It's very easy to get there. Get off the bus in Prince Street. Walk up Prince Street. Turn right into Bridge Street. Then go across Thames Grove and turn left into Church Road. Sports Plus is on the corner of Church Road and West Street.

Jessy: Will it be on my left or on my right?

Emma: It'll be on your left.

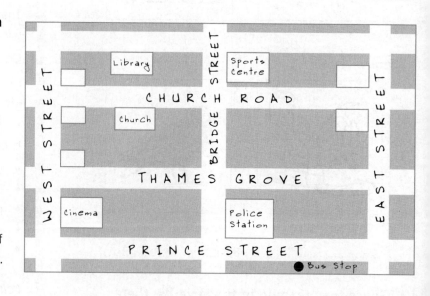

Let's check

1 **Choose the correct word for each sentence.**

She walked ..into.............. the room and everyone looked at her.

(**A** into)   **B** up   **C** under

1 My brother swam .... that river last summer.

A past   **B** across   **C** under

2 We climbed .... the gate and looked at the old house.

A over   **B** past   **C** into

3 They walked .... the mountain.

A up   **B** under   **C** through

4 Don't go .... the cave. It's full of spiders.

A over   **B** across   **C** into

5 I don't like walking .... that house. There's a horrible dog in the garden.

A past   **B** along   **C** up

6 Come and stand .... my umbrella.

A under   **B** through   **C** along

7 This bus goes .... the cinema. Let's get it.

A along   **B** into   **C** towards

8 I don't like walking up mountains. I like walking .... them.

A into   **B** down   **C** through

9 Let's walk .... the forest today.

A up   **B** down   **C** through

10 Cycle .... this path and you'll get to the lake.

A into   **B** along   **C** through

2 **Correct the sentences by deleting one word in each sentence.**

Could I ~~to~~ borrow this book from you, please?

1 The king lived there 200 years back ago.

2 Who did left all these books on my desk?

3 Don't to turn left after the bridge.

4 Turn the right at the roundabout.

5 We were found this money in the street.

3 **Put the words in order, to make sentences.**

ago / bought / CD player / I / my / two / years

I bought my CD player two years ago.

1 buy / car / did / father / When / that / your / ?

....

....

2 and / at / go / left / roundabout / straight on / the / Turn.

....

....

3 and / bridge / Go over / on / second / take / the / the / turning / the right

....

....

4 an hour / bike / borrow / Could / for / half / I / your

....

....

5 Could / me / post office / tell / the / the / to / way / you / ?

....

....

4 **Choose the correct word.**

She got it .a.year.ago......... .

A ago a year   **B** a year   (**C** a year ago)

1 Where .... those shoes?

A bought you   **B** you did buy   **C** did you buy

2 Who .... my bike here?

A put   **B** did leave   **C** leave

3 Could I .... your phone?

A use   **B** using   **C** used

4 .... the first turning.

A Go   **B** Turn   **C** Take

5 The cinema's .... the left.

A turn   **B** on   **C** your

1 Read the text and answer the questions.

Luke Watson is not an ordinary 3-year old. Last July, he saved his mother's life ...

When three-year-old Luke Watson woke up on July 15th, he was worried. Usually his mother woke up before him and came into his room, but that Monday she wasn't there. And there was no noise from her bedroom. He got up quickly and went to his mother's room. He found his mother, Andrea, in her bed. She was sleeping so he tried to wake her up. He pushed her, pulled the covers off her, called her name. But still she didn't wake up.

Andrea is a diabetic. Sometimes the level of sugar in her blood drops too low. Luke knows this and he knows the right thing to do. So that Monday, he went to look for his mother's "medicine". It's a fizzy drink with a lot of sugar in it. When Andrea's blood sugar drops too low, she always drinks some of it.

Luke brought the bottle to his mother's bedroom and tried to give it to her. But Andrea didn't wake up. So Luke picked up the phone and dialled 999.

Emergency operator, Carol Ellis answered Luke's call. "He was very calm. He said, 'My mum's asleep. I can't wake her up.' I asked him for his address and he told me the house number and the name of the street. We sent an ambulance immediately."

When the ambulance arrived at his house, Luke stood on a chair and opened the door for the paramedics. They ran upstairs, found Andrea. and gave her an injection. She woke up very quickly.

"Luke saved my life," Andrea says. "He's a clever, calm child. I'm really proud of him."

1 How old was Luke?

2 Why was he worried when he woke up that Monday?

3 How did he try to wake his mother up?

4 What is wrong with Andrea?

5 What does Andrea usually take when her blood sugar drops too low?

6 What did Luke take to his mother's room?

7 Why didn't she take it?

8 What number did Luke call?

9 What information did Carol Ellis ask him for?

10 How did the paramedics get into Luke's house?

11 What do you do when you feel ill?

12 Describe in two sentences a young child that you like.

Answers

1 ....

2 ....

....

3 ....

4 ....

5 ....

6 ....

7 ....

8 ....

9 ....

10 ....

....

11 ....

....

....

12 ....

....

....

2 Read the article about a dancer. Are sentences 1 to 10 'Right' (A) or 'Wrong' (B)? If there's not enough information to answer 'Right' or 'Wrong', choose 'Doesn't say' (C).

This week our interviewer talks to the dancer Sylvie Chevalier.

You started dancing at six, didn't you?

That's right. I went to a class in my village. There were only five of us in the class and I was the youngest. I decided then to become a dancer.

At what age did you go to the Royal Ballet School?

I got a place there when I was eleven.

How did they choose you?

I went to the ballet school with my mother for a sort of exam.

An exam? What was that like?

Well, I danced in front of six people. Then they asked me questions. Somebody looked at my feet and my back. And then I went home with my mother. I didn't expect to get a place.

But you did. You got a place at the Royal Ballet School and you studied there for six years.

That's right. We did normal school subjects half the day and we danced half the day.

Did you enjoy your years at ballet school?

Yes, I did. But we worked very hard. I never had any free time. And I was always very careful about food.

What do you mean?

Well, dancers mustn't get fat or be too heavy. So I never ate cakes, sweets or chocolate. I never drank fizzy drinks. And I'm still very careful about my diet.

You stopped doing ballet three years ago. Why was that?

Well, I wanted to try something new. I wanted to try modern dance. And I was interested in acting.

And what do you do now – acting or dancing?

Both! I've got a part as a dancer in a film called *Hollywood*.

EXAMPLE

0 Sylvie started dancing at the age of seven.

A Right   (B Wrong)   C Doesn't say

1 Sylvie once lived in a village.

A Right   B Wrong   C Doesn't say

2 She was the youngest student at the Royal Ballet School.

A Right   B Wrong   C Doesn't say

3 She was very nervous at the exam.

A Right   B Wrong   C Doesn't say

4 Sylvie's father took her to her ballet audition.

A Right   B Wrong   C Doesn't say

5 She didn't expect to get a place at the Royal Ballet School.

A Right   B Wrong   C Doesn't say

6 The students only studied dance at the ballet school.

A Right   B Wrong   C Doesn't say

7 Sylvie didn't enjoy life at the Royal Ballet School.

A Right   B Wrong   C Doesn't say

8 Sylvie is very careful about food.

A Right   B Wrong   C Doesn't say

9 Sylvie doesn't do any dancing now.

A Right   B Wrong   C Doesn't say

10 Sylvie dances with lots of other dancers in the film *Hollywood*.

A Right   B Wrong   C Doesn't say

GRAMMAR FILE

Past continuous

Affirmative

I was sitting.
You were sitting.
She/He/It was sitting.
We were sitting.
You were sitting.
They were sitting.

Negative

I wasn't working.
You weren't working.
She/He/It wasn't working.
We weren't working.
You weren't working.
They weren't working.

Questions

Was I running?
Were you running?
Was she/he/it running?
Were we running?
Were you running?
Were they running?

Short answers

Affirmative	Negative
Yes, I was.	No, I wasn't.
Yes, you were.	No, you weren't.
Yes, she/he/it was.	No, she/he/it wasn't.
Yes, we were.	No, we weren't.
Yes, they were.	No, they weren't.

- We use the Past continuous for an action that was happening at a definite time in the past, e.g. *At five o'clock I was doing my homework in my bedroom. It wasn't raining at three o'clock. What were you doing yesterday morning?*
- We often use the Past continuous and the Past simple in the same sentence. We use the Past continuous for the background activity or situation and the Past simple for the shorter action, e.g. *I was sitting in the garden when I saw a beautiful bird. While she was swimming, somebody took her clothes.*
- We form the Past continuous with *was/were* + present participle (*-ing* form) of the verb.
- There are rules for forming the present participle:
  We usually add *-ing* to the verb, e.g. *read/reading, walk/walking, go/going, play/playing.*
  With verbs ending in one *e*, we drop the *e* and add *-ing*, e.g. *ride – riding, write – writing.*
  With one-syllable verbs that end in one vowel and one consonant (NOT *w* or *y*), we double the last consonant and add *-ing*, e.g. *run – running, sit –sitting, swim – swimming, get – getting.*

Reflexive pronouns

Subject pronoun	Reflexive pronouns
I	myself
you	yourself
she	herself
he	himself
it	itself
we	ourselves
you	yourselves
they	themselves

- We use a reflexive pronoun as the object in a sentence when the subject and the object refer to the same person or animal, e.g. *Be careful. Don't cut yourself with that knife. She looked at herself in the mirror and smiled.*

I didn't enjoy **myself** at the party.
Why are you looking at **yourself** in the mirror?
How did she hurt **herself**?
He fell over and cut **himself**.
Does this CD player turn **itself** off?
Can we help **ourselves** to sandwiches?
Yes, please help **yourselves**.
They saw **themselves** on TV.

- We can also use *myself, yourself,* etc to emphasize a personal pronoun, e.g. *I made this cake myself* (= nobody helped me), *He didn't do it himself* (= somebody helped him). *Maria was there. We saw her ourselves* (= we know this not because somebody told us, but because we saw her there).

- The ending is *-self* for singular reflexive pronouns and *-selves* for plural reflexive pronouns. We use *yourself* for one person and *yourselves* for more than one person, e.g. *Do it yourself, Jamie. Joey and Maria, you must do this yourselves.*

Were you chatting up boys?

Vocabulary

1 **Write the numbers 1–20 next to the correct words.**

beard .....13..........   forehead ....   long nails ....   spiky hair ....

cheek ....   freckles ....   mole ....   straight hair ....

chin ....   fringe ....   moustache ....   teeth ....

ear ....   glasses ....   nose ....   tongue ....

eye ....   lips ....   scar ....   wavy hair ....

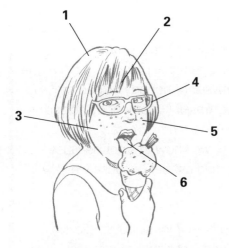

Dialogue work

2 **Complete the dialogue with the sentences below.**

Sophie	What were you doing yesterday after school?
Kate	What time?
Sophie	Around five o'clock.
Kate	(1) ....
Sophie	I phoned, but you didn't answer.
Kate	(2) ....
Sophie	Why not?
Kate	(3) ....
Sophie	Do you often do your homework in the bath?
Kate	(4) ....
Sophie	What homework were you doing?
Kate	(5) ....

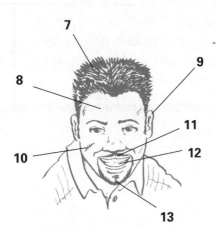

- No, but yesterday I did.
- I was at home. Why?
- Sorry. I didn't hear the phone.
- Spanish. I was sitting in the bath and listening to a Spanish programme on the radio.
- Well at five o'clock I was having a bath and doing my homework.
- ~~What time?~~

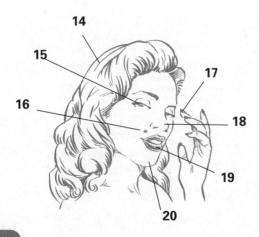

Grammar practice

3 Choose the correct form to complete the sentences

I (was)/ were) thinking about you.

1 She (was / were) wearing her new earrings yesterday.

2 Sam and Joey (was / were) talking about the band.

3 What (was / were) you doing yesterday at five?

4 Don't worry. We (was / were) only joking.

5 I (was / were) looking at something in the newspaper.

6 They (was / were) feeling tired.

7 What (was / were) he telling you?

8 You (was / were) laughing at me, I know it.

4 Put the sentences in the negative.

I was wearing jeans yesterday.

I wasn't wearing jeans yesterday.

1 We were talking about music.

....

....

2 Sandra was playing her guitar.

....

....

3 Josh and Luke were getting angry.

....

....

4 Maria was reading a magazine in class.

....

....

5 My parents were watching TV at ten o'clock.

....

....

6 Kate was laughing about the detention.

....

....

7 Biba was feeling hungry.

....

....

8 Sven was doing his homework.

....

....

5 Write sentences in the Past continuous.

Mark (✗) play tennis. He (✓) play football

Mark wasn't playing tennis.

He was playing football.

1 I (✗) talk to you. I (✓) talk to Angela.

....

....

2 We (✗) walk. We (✓) run.

....

....

3 I (✓) listen to the radio. I (✗) watch TV.

....

....

4 They (✓) laugh at a joke. They (✗) laugh at you.

....

....

5 You (✗) wear your blue jacket. You (✓) wear your green one.

....

....

6 Maria (✗) sing. She (✓) play the guitar.

....

....

7 Tom (✓) write. He (✗) draw on the desk.

....

....

8 We (✓) make pancakes. We (✗) make milkshakes.

....

....

6 Read the clues and complete the chart. Then write what each person was doing and where they were. Everyone was doing something different.

	Adam	Beth	Carlos	Diane
taking photos		✗		
skating		✗		
running				
listening to a CD				
in the park				
in Lime Street				
near the lake				
on the beach road				

- Beth doesn't have skates or a camera.
- Carlos went out with his camera.
- Diane can't skate. She is only interested in music.
- Adam hates running. He was near water.
- One person was taking photos of the sea.
- The person with the CD player was sitting on the grass under a tree.
- The runner was in the middle of the town.

Adam was .... ing in/on/near

....

....

Beth ....

....

....

Carlos ....

....

....

Diane ....

....

....

7 Complete the dialogues using the Past continuous.

Why ..were you singing........... (you / sing) in the shower?

I ...wasn't singing....................... (not sing).

Yes, you were.................................. (✓)

No, .I wasn't................................ (✗).

I ..was listening........................... (listen) to the radio.

1 A: Who .... (you / talk) to in the kitchen?

B: I .... (not talk) to anyone.

A: Yes, ... (you / ✓)

B: No, ... (I / ✗).

I .... (talk) to myself.

2 A: Why... (you / look) at your watch just now?

B: I .... (not look) at my watch.

A: Yes, ... (you / ✓)

B: No, ... (I / ✗).

Look! I'm not wearing my watch today!

3 A: What .... (Amy / do) in the park yesterday?

B: She .... (run).

She's in the school athletics team.

A: She .... (not run).

B: Yes, ... (she / ✓)

A: I saw her. She .... (walk).

4 A: What .... (you / look) at on the internet just now?

B: I ....

(not / look) at anything.

A: Yes, ... (you / ✓)

B: No, ... (I / ✗).

I ....

(write) an e-mail to Harry.

8 Complete the dialogues using the Past continuous.

do	read	sit	~~stand~~	wait	wear
look	ride	skate	take	walk	wear

Police File

Police officer	You .....were standing...... at the bus stop yesterday morning when there was an accident. Can you tell us anything about it?
Max	I (1) .... for the bus. An old woman (2) .... across the street. She (3) .... a big hat and she had a little dog. A bike hit her.
Police officer	Who (4) .... the bike?
Max	I didn't know him.
Police officer	What (5) .... he ....?
Max	Jeans and a white jacket.
Police officer	Can you tell me about the other people in the street? What were they doing?
Max	A girl on roller blades (6) .... towards the bus stop. And a man (7) .... in his car. (8) He .... a newspaper. Two girls (9) .... in a shop window. And there was a boy with a camera.
Police officer	What (10) .... he ....?
Max	He (11) .... photos.
Police officer	Excellent. Perhaps he's got a photo of the accident.

9 Match the sentence halves.

1 Did you make this [b]
2 Did Alice burn [ ]
3 Please make yourselves [ ]
4 Can you lend me a comb? I just [ ]
5 He fell off his bike in the park [ ]
6 I'm making a film of the party so we [ ]
7 This story is amazing. Did you [ ]
8 He's a bit crazy. He always [ ]
9 The CD player will [ ]

a) and hurt himself.
b) ~~birthday card yourself?~~
c) can watch ourselves later on the video.
d) herself on the barbecue?
e) saw myself in the bathroom mirror.
f) some coffee.
g) turn itself off.
h) talks to himself.
i) write it yourself?

Skills development

Read

1 **Read the first part of the story and find the answers to these questions.**

1 Where does the story take place?

....

2 What time of year was it?

....

3 How old was the little girl?

....

4 What did she have around her neck?

....

The Girl at the Lake

This is a **true** story. My name's Dylan Mathews and I'm an **artist**. Last year I was living in Wales near a lake. I had a little house and a small **boat** for **fishing** on the lake. One afternoon I was in my house. It was summer and the door was open. I was sitting near the window and I was **painting a picture** of the lake. Suddenly, I heard a noise behind me. I looked around. There was a little girl in my room. I didn't know her. She was about nine years old. She was wearing a **gold** necklace with the letter M on it.

2 **Read the second part and write T (true) or F (false).**

'Please,' she said. 'My name's Martha and I need your help. Now. My sister Katrin is in the lake. She's sixteen but she isn't a very good **swimmer**. The lake is very dangerous and my sister is very tired. She's going to **drown**. Please hurry.' Then she ran out of the house.

1 Katrin was Martha's sister.   [ ]

2 Katrin was 14.   [ ]

3 Katrin was a very good swimmer.   [ ]

4 The lake was very dangerous.   [ ]

5 Katrin needed help.   [ ]

3 **Read the third part of the story and put the events in order by numbering them.**

a) Katrin said thank you.   [ ]

b) Dylan ran out of the house.   [1]

c) He brought Katrin home.   [ ]

d) He called a doctor.   [ ]

e) He found Katrin.   [ ]

f) He got Katrin out of the lake. [ ]

g) He took his boat on the lake. [ ]

I ran out of the house too. I didn't see the little girl anywhere. So I got into my boat and went to the middle of the lake. Suddenly I saw something in the water. It was Katrin. She wasn't swimming. Her head was under the water. I pulled her out and took her back to my house. I gave her a hot drink and phoned a doctor. 'Thank you,' she said.

4 Read the last part of the story and fill in the missing words and phrases.

don't	haven't got	her name	in this lake
looked at	must	neck	nine years old
~~thank you~~		two years ago	

.....'Thank you.'..... . Katrin said. 'You saved my life.' '(1) .... thank me,' I said, 'You (2) .... thank your sister. She came and got me.' Suddenly Katrin started to **cry**.

'I (3) .... a sister,' she said. 'My sister **died** (4) .... She was only (5) .... Look. This was her necklace.' I (6) .... the necklace around Katrin's (7) .... It was gold and it had the letter M on it.

'What was (8) ....,' I asked.

'Martha,' Katrin answered. 'She died (9)............................. . She fell in and drowned.'

Study tips

You don't always need to look words up in a dictionary. You can sometimes work out the meaning.

- **Some words are very similar in English and other languages, for example** *artist, music, football, tennis.*

- **Some words are like words you already know. For example,** *fishing* **and** *swimming* **are like** *fish* **and** *swim.*

- **Sometimes you can guess a word from the context, for example,** *I'm an artist ... I was painting a picture.*

5 Guess the meaning of these words. Then check in a dictionary.

1 true ....
2 artist ....
3 boat...
4 fishing ....
5 paint a picture ....
6 gold...
7 swimmer ....
8 drown ....
9 cry ....
10 die..

Write

6 Write the rest of the conversation between Dylan and Katrin. Start like this. Write six more lines.

Dylan .But Martha came to my house an hour ago....

Katrin .What do you mean?................................

Dylan ....
....

Katrin ....
....

Dylan ....
....

Katrin ....
....

Dylan ....
....

Katrin ....
....

1 **Put the sentences in order by numbering them 1 to 6.**

[ ] Could you tell me the way to the Waterview Cinema?

[ ] Excuse me, do you know this town?

[ ] Is it far?

[ ] It's quite a long way.

[ ] Yes. Go straight on and take the first left.

[ ] Yes. I live here.

2 **Write the phrases in the balloons.**

- I don't care.
- I was only joking.
- Oh, I see.
- That's why
- Why are you late home?

It's ten in the morning.
....

Do you really think I'm dirty?

Of course I don't.
....

The water's a bit warm but
....
I'm going swimming anywa

I'm a vegetarian. I don't eat meat.

....

....
she's always late for school.

Let's check

1 **Write the words next to the clues.**

You eat with them. t <u>e</u> <u>e</u> <u>t</u> <u>h</u>

1 You hear with them. e _ _ _

2 You see with them. e _ _ _

3 You put food in it. m _ _ _ _

4 You need it to speak. t _ _ _ _ _

5 Some men have one on their chin. b _ _ _ <u>d</u>

6 Some people need them to see. g _ _ _ _ _ <u>s</u>

7 It can be curly, wavy or long, for example.

h _ _ _

8 Some men have one over their top lip.

m _ _ _ _ _ <u>c</u> <u>h</u> <u>e</u>

9 Fair skinned people with red hair often have these.

f _ _ <u>c</u> <u>k</u> _ _ <u>s</u>

10 It's the opposite of fair skinned.

d _ _ <u>k</u> s _ _ _ _ _ d.

2 **Choose the correct words.**

Don't worry about my supper. I'll make it ...<u>myself</u>..

A me   B herself   Ⓒ myself

1 She didn't buy those trousers. She made
them ....

A themselves B herself C itself

2 I'm not going to do this for you. Do it ....

A itself   B herself   C yourself

3 I .... thinking about Amy this morning.

A was   B were   C is

4 We really enjoyed .... at the party.

A ourself   B ourselves   C us

5 What .... doing in the kitchen at midnight?

A he was   B was he   C did he

6 'Was she going fast when she fell off her bike?'
'No, she ....'

A wasn't   B didn't   C isn't

7 Help .... to some cake, all of you.

A yourselves B yourself C itself

8 They .... wearing ridiculous hats at the match.

A wasn't   B didn't   C were

3 **Write sentences in the Past continuous.**

We (talk) about the film.

<u>We were talking about the film.</u>

1 James and I (take) photos all day yesterday.

....

....

2 I (not read) a magazine in class. I (write) a story.

....

....

3 She (not look) at me. She (look) at you.

....

....

4 What (they / do) with that box of magazines?

....

....

5 Where (you / go) with Sam yesterday?

....

....

4 **Complete the dialogues using the Past continuous.**

A: <u>Were Josh and Dan playing</u> (Josh and
Dan / play) in the match?

B: No, <u>they weren't</u>.............. (they / ✗). They
<u>were watching</u>..................... . (watch) it.

1 A: What .... (you / do)?

B: I .... (write) something.

A: .... (you / write)
on the desk?

B: No, ... (I / ✗).

2 A: What ....
(you read) in that magazine?

B: I............................... (not read) anything.

A: Yes, ... (you /✓)

B: No. I .... (look)
at the photos of clothes.

GRAMMAR FILE

would like to

Would you like to come to my party on Saturday?
Yes, I would. / Yes, I'd love to. / Yes, I'd really like to.
I'm sorry, I can't. / I'm afraid I can't.
What would you like to do tomorrow?
I'd like to go sightseeing.
Where would you like to go?
I'd like to go for a boat trip on the Thames.

- We use questions with *would .... like (to)* for offers, e.g. *What would you like to drink? Would you like to watch a video? Would they like a sandwich?*
- We can't write the short form *'d* in questions, e.g. *When would you like to leave?* NOT ~~*When'd you like to leave?*~~
- To refuse an offer, we use phrases like *I'm sorry, I can't* OR: *No, thanks.*

Adverbs of manner

Regular adverbs

bad	badly
quick	quickly
slow	slowly
quiet	quietly
careful	carefully
dangerous	dangerously
easy	easily
noisy	noisily

Irregular adverbs

good	well
hard	hard
fast	fast
early	early
late	late

- We use adverbs of manner to describe how actions are done, e.g. *He drives dangerously. She sings beautifully.*
- To form most adverbs of manner, we add *-ly* to the end of an adjective, e.g. *slow/slowly, careful/carefully, nice/nicely.*
- With adjectives ending in a consonant + *-y*, we drop the *y* and add *-ily*, e.g. *noisy/noisily, easy/easily, angry/angrily.*
- There are some irregular adverbs, e.g. *good/well, late/late.* We say: *She skis well* NOT ~~*She skis goodly.*~~ *The bus arrived late* NOT ~~*The bus arrived lately.*~~
- An adverb of manner usually comes after the object of the verb, e.g. *She wrote the letter slowly.* If there isn't an object, the adverb comes after the verb, e.g. *She wrote slowly.*

whose?

Whose is this jacket?
Whose are these keys?
Whose jacket is this?
Whose keys are these?

- We use *whose* to ask who is the owner of something, e.g. *Whose bag is that? Whose is that bag?*
- *Whose* can be an adjective and come next to a noun, e.g. *Whose bike were you riding yesterday?* Or it can be a pronoun, e.g. *Whose is that bike?*

Present simple and Present continuous (revision)

Present simple
What do you usually do at the weekend?
I usually go out with my friends.
I don't get up early on Saturdays.

- We use the Present simple for permanent situations and routines, e.g. *She lives in Australia. I get up at seven.*
- We often use adverbs of frequency with the Present simple, e.g. *I never stay up late on weekdays. Do you ever play tennis in winter?*
- We also use the Present simple to talk about things that generally happen, e.g. *It rains a lot in November.*

Present continuous
What are you doing at the moment?
I'm lying in bed and listening to my new CD.
I'm not doing my homework at the moment.

Present continuous for future
What are you doing next weekend?
I'm taking Julian to a football match.
I'm not taking Charlie to the match.

- We use the Present continuous for actions which are happening at the moment when we are speaking, e.g. *Ssh! I'm watching a really interesting TV programme.*
- We also use it to talk about actions which are happening during the present period, e.g. *What are you studying in History at the moment?*
- We also use the Present continuous to talk about fixed arrangements for the future, especially when we say the time, e.g. *Soraya is arriving at eleven. Adam isn't coming to school tomorrow. What time are you leaving on Sunday?*

Past simple and Past continuous (revision)

Past simple
What did you watch on TV last night?
We watched a music programme.
We didn't watch the James Bond film.

Past continuous
What were you doing at six o'clock yesterday evening?
I was watching TV.
I wasn't talking on the phone.
I was watching TV when I heard a strange noise in the kitchen.

- We use the Past simple for actions that happened at a definite time in the past. We often use it with time expressions like *yesterday, last week, two months ago, last April, in the summer, in 2001,* e.g. *We saw her two months ago. I didn't go to the beach last week.*
- We use the Past continuous for an action that was happening at a definite time in the past, e.g. *Last Saturday afternoon Martin was watching the match on TV. What were you doing on Saturday afternoon?*
- We often use the Past continuous and the Past simple in the same sentence. We use the Past continuous for the background activity or situation and the Past simple for the shorter action, e.g. *I was having a shower when the telephone rang.*

Would you like to meet Liberty X ?

Vocabulary

1 **Write the numbers 1 to 14 next to the correct words.**

bracelet .....10...........	mobile phone ....
camera	necklace ....
CD player	purse ....
comb	skateboard ....
diary	sunglasses ....
earrings	watch ....
key ring	wallet ....

Dialogue work

2 **Complete the dialogue with the sentences below.**

Kate Would you like to see the new James Bond film tonight?

Ashan Yes, I'd love to. ....

Kate Sophie and Alex are coming too.

Ashan (1) ....

Kate No, but I've got free tickets.

Ashan (2) ....

Kate One of the girls at the XL Cinema.

Ashan (3) ....

Kate I was walking past the cinema last night and she was giving free tickets to everyone.

Ashan (4) ....
....

Kate Four. She gave me two but I asked her for two more!

- Is it your birthday or something?
- Lucky you! How many did she give you?
- Who gave them to you?
- Why did she give them to you?
- ~~Yes, I'd love to.~~

104

Grammar practice

3 **Match the sentences to the phrases below. Then write sentences with *Would you like to*.**

It's a lovely hot day. [c]

Would you like to come to the beach with us?

1 Are you OK? [ ] ....
....

2 I'm going for a run. [ ] ....
....

3 These are my new skates. [ ] ....
....

4 I'm making a cake. [ ] ....
....

5 I've got a new S Club CD. [ ] ....
....

6 My cousin has got tickets. [ ] ....
....

7 I'm not wearing my green top tonight. [ ] ....
....

8 Your hair looks a bit wild. [ ] ....
....

a) borrow a comb?
b) buy one from him?
c) ~~come to the beach with us?~~
d) come with me?
e) hear it?
f) help me?
g) sit down for a moment?
h) try them?
i) wear it?

4 **Complete the dialogues. Include the phrases *would you like* and *I'd like*. Add an appropriate verb where necessary.**

Q: What would you like to do... tomorrow?

A: I'd like. to go for a picnic.

Q: Where (**1**) ....?

A: To the lake.

Q: When (**2**) ....?

A: Let's leave at about eleven.

Q: Would you like to ask.... anyone else?

A: Why don't we ask Sophie and Ashan?

Q: What (**3**).....................................
at the weekend?

A: On Saturday (**4**) ....
for a bike ride.

Q: Where (**5**) ....?

A: Let's cycle all around Richmond Park.

Q: What about Sunday?

A: (**6**) .... some videos.

Q: Which ones (**7**) ....
...........................?

A: (**8**) .... all the Indiana Jones ones.

Q: (**9**) ....
invite some friends round?

A: Yes. Ben and Georgia.

Q: What (**10**) ....
on your birthday?

A: Have a barbecue.

Q: Where (**11**) ....
.... it?

A: On the beach.

5 **Make the adjectives into adverbs.**

quick	quickly
fast	fast
1 early	....
2 dangerous	....
3 hard	....
4 late	....
5 quiet	....
6 safe	....
7 slow	....
8 good	....

6 **Use each adverb in Exercise 5 once to complete these sentences.**

1 She sings really .... She's the best singer in our class.

2 I did my homework ..quickly.. then took the dog out for a walk.

3 He's a very bad driver. He drives really ....

4 We opened the door .... because we didn't want to wake them up.

5 We were late so Dad drove very ...fast........ .

6 We arrived .... so we didn't have time for supper.

7 It was a hot day and we were tired so we walked up the mountain ....

8 I'm never frightened on the motorbike with her. She drives very ....

9 We arrived .... so we had to wait for Meg and Emma outside the cinema.

10 You always work ....

7 **Write the verbs in the Present simple or Present continuous.**

We use the Present continuous to talk about
- things that are happening now
- fixed arrangements for the future

This is my friend Anna. She ....lives... (live) in my street but she **(1)** .... (go) to a different school. She **(2)** .... (read) a lot and **(3)** .... (write) really good stories in her school magazine. In this photo she **(4)** .... (act) Father Christmas in the school play. She **(5)** .... (not like) this photo but I **(6)** .... (think) it's great!

This is Matt. He's in a different year at school but I **(7)** .... (see) him every day. We usually **(8)** .... (take) the same bus to school. Matt always **(9)** .... (invite) me to his birthday parties and he usually **(10)** .... (come) to mine. This weekend he **(11)** .... (have) a party on the beach. Everyone **(12)** .... (bring) some food and drink and two CDs. In this photo Matt **(13)** .... (play) his guitar in his bedroom. His room **(14)** .... (be) always very messy. He **(15)** .... (not tidy) it very often.

This is Sabrina. She's my cousin. She (**16**) …….……… (not live) in London but she often (**17**) ………….…..…… (stay) with us in the summer. This summer she (**18**) …………….……..……… (spend) two weeks with us in London, then we (**19**) ………….…..………… (go) camping together in Dorset. Sabrina (**20**) ……….…..… (have got) a beautiful horse called Snowball. She's a very good rider. I (**21**) ………….……. (not ride) but Sabrina (**22**) ………….……… (want) to teach me. In this photo, Sabrina (**23**) ……………………… (sit) on Snowball. She (**24**)…………………… (not look) at the camera because she (**25**)…………..……… (not like) being in photos.

8 Put the correct verb in the correct tense: Past simple or Past continuous.

> She (hear / read) her magazine, when she (hear / read) a strange noise.
>
> *She was reading her magazine when she*
> *heard a strange noise.*

1 I (stand / see) at the bus stop when I (stand / see) a big green bird.

....
....

2 Sara (find / go) to school when she (find / go) £20 in the street.

....
....

3 I (drop / run) to the station when I (drop / run) my phone.

....
....

4 How fast (he fall / he ride) when he (fall / ride) off his bike?

....
....

5 I (have / phone) a shower when somebody (have / phone).

....
....

9 Put the verbs in the Present simple, Past simple or Past continuous.

I ...like.... (like) animals a lot but my cat Milly sometimes (**1**) …………… (make) me really angry. For example, last week I (**2**) ……………… (hurt) my leg badly because of my cat. I usually (**3**) …………… (go) to bed at ten o'clock but last Thursday I (**4**) …………… (go) to bed at midnight. I (**5**) ……………………… (lie) in bed when I suddenly (**6**) …………… (hear) a strange noise in the garden. I (**7**) …………… (get) out of bed quickly and (**8**)…………… (run) to the window. I (**9**) …………… (open) it and (**10**) ……………… (look) out. My cat Milly (**11**) …………………… (sit) in a tree very near my bedroom window. Two other cats (**12**) ……………………… (stand) on the grass under the tree and they (**13**) ………..……………… (screech). 'Be quiet,' I shouted. But the cats on the grass (**14**) …………………….. (not stop) screeching. And Milly suddenly (**15**) …………… (jump) from the tree into my room. I (**16**) …………… (fall) back and (**17**) …………… (hit) a chair. I (**18**) …………… (cut) my leg. My mother (**19**) …………… (run) into my room. 'Are you OK?' she asked. 'Yes,' I (**20**)………………… (answer). 'I fell over because a minute ago Milly (**21**) ………………… (fly) through the window,' I (**22**) ………………… (tell) her. 'Don't be ridiculous, Annabel,' she (**23**) ……………………… (say). 'Cats (**24**) ………………… (not fly).'

Culture spot

Holiday in the USA

New ▼ | Send | Receive | Forward | Delete

Hi Jamie

(1) ....

Yesterday we took the **ferry** to Liberty Island and visited the Statue of Liberty. I took lots of photos. Then, in the afternoon, we went to the top of the Empire State building. (2) ....

The **skyscrapers** are higher than all the buildings in London. Tomorrow we're going on a **helicopter** ride over New York. I'm really looking forward to it.

Bye Laura

New ▼ | Send | Receive | Forward | Delete

Hi Sandro

Why don't you come and visit us in California this summer? (3) ....
....

Dad would like to take us camping in Yosemite. There are **bears** there, but don't worry! We'll be careful. You can also see the biggest trees in the world there – they're called Giant Redwoods. My mom wants to take us **whale** watching. I went whale watching last year and I saw a whale. It was **awesome**. It was swimming in the ocean next to the boat (4) ....

Why don't you get on a plane next week?

See you soon!

Scott :) :)

New ▼ | Send | Receive | Forward | Delete

Jessica, you must come here one day. There's lots to see and do in Florida. Yesterday (5)...

It's full of interesting **wildlife** – alligators (they're American crocodiles), birds and snakes. There are also a lot of horrible **insects**! We were looking at some green **plants** in the forest and then one of the plants climbed quickly up a tree. It was a green snake, not a plant! This morning we went out in a boat to look at fish. We sat in the boat and watched the fish through the glass bottom of the boat.

(6) ....

Lots of love Marianne xxxxx

1 Read the texts. Write these sentences in the correct gaps.

- Mom, Dad and I really want you to come.
- New York is the most exciting city in the world.
- The view was fantastic.
- They were beautiful – all different colours.
- We went to the Everglade National Park.
- and it was about 10 metres long.

2 Match the captions to the pictures.

a) A bear in Yosemite National Park.

b) An alligator in the Everglades.

c) The view from the Empire State building.

d) You get to Liberty Island by ferry.

Vocabulary

3 Guess what these words mean. Then check in the dictionary.

1 ferry ....
2 skyscraper ....
3 helicopter ....
4 bear ....
5 whale ....
6 wildlife ....
7 insects ....
8 plants ....

4 Can you guess what *awesome* is in British English?

A amazing   **B** horrible   **C** stupid

Portfolio

5 Write about you and places you'd like to visit.

1 Which country would you most like to visit?
   ....
2 Who would you like to go with?
   ....
3 How long would you like to stay there?
   ....
4 Which city would you most like to visit?
   ....
5 What do you want to see/do in that city? Name three things.
   ....
   ....
   ....
6 Name another city/place you'd like to go to. Give a reason.
   I'd also like to go to ....
   because ....

Let's read

Enjoy your trip

• evenings	• minutes	• tickets
• exciting	• ~~most famous~~	• times
• information	• number	• trip
• leave	• office	

1 Choose the correct words for the gaps.

BIG APPLE HELICOPTERS

NEW YORK'S <u>most famous</u>......... HELICOPTER SIGHTSEEING COMPANY

Take a trip on one of our helicopters and you'll have the most
(1) ....…............. day of your vacation:

You can choose from these (2) ....:

Mornings:	8.30	and	10.00	
Afternoons:	2.00	and	3.30	
(3)	6.00	and	9.00	

Each trip is fifteen **(4)** ....…................ .

Our helicopters **(5)** ....…............... from the River Heliport.

You can get to the heliport by bus **(6)** ....…............... G37.

All **(7)** ....…............. are $70.

For more (8) ....…............ **call us now on 6462300395.**

Or come into our (9) ....…............... **at 411 East 45th Street.**

Enjoy your (10) ....…............ **and thank you for calling
Big Apple Helicopters.**

Let's check

1 **Which words from each column go together? Match them and write them under the pictures. Where necessary join the pairs of words.**

CD	[d]	**a)** board
1 ear	[ ]	**b)** glasses
2 key	[ ]	**c)** phone
3 mobile	[ ]	**d)** ~~player~~
4 skate	[ ]	**e)** ring
5 sun	[ ]	**f)** ring

....

....

....

..CD player...........

....

....

2 **Choose the correct words.**

I was late so I cycled very ...**fast**...... .

A slowly   **B** fast   **C** easily

1 Why .... looking at that photo yesterday?

  A were you   **B** are you   **C** did you

2 She .... her lunch. She wasn't hungry.

  A isn't eating   **B** didn't eat   **C** doesn't eat

3 What .... to have for dinner?

  A would you like   **B** are you like   **C** want you

4 We always .... to Scotland in the summer.

  A are going   **B** were going   **C** go

5 I'd like .... your holiday photos.

  A see   **B** I see   **C** to see

6 I always get into the swimming pool ....

  A slow   **B** very slow   **C** slowly

3 **Choose the correct words.**

I am (feeling / was feeling) hungry so I made a sandwich.

1 Where were you going when I (see / saw) you yesterday?

2 Please be quiet. We (are doing / do) our homework.

3 What (do you do / did you do) when you heard the news?

4 'Why (do you wear / are you wearing) those old clothes today?' 'Because (I'm helping / I help) my parents in the garden at the moment.'

5 Ssh! My little sister (sleeps / is sleeping).

4 **Write the verbs in the Present simple, Present continuous, Past simple or Past continuous.**

My cat (usually sleep) in the kitchen but last night she (sleep) on my bed.

> My cat usually sleeps in the kitchen but....... last night she slept on my bed.....................

1 Last week I (walk) to school when I (see) a very strange bird.

....
....

2 Dan usually (wear) an earring but today he (not wear) one.

....
....

3 Yesterday, we (stand) in the garden when we (hear) a loud noise.

....
....

4 My mother usually (cycle) to work but yesterday she (take) the bus.

....
....

Extra!

1 **Read the text and answer the questions.**

J K Rowling got her idea for Harry Potter on a long train trip in 1990. The train was late and Rowling didn't have anything to do. So she started to make up characters for a book. She was working as a secretary then so she didn't have time to work seriously on the book.

In 1992, Rowling moved to Portugal to teach English. She wrote in the mornings and taught in the afternoons and evenings. Then she got married and had a daughter – Jessica. The marriage wasn't happy and ended in divorce. Rowling moved back to Britain with Jessica and a suitcase full of notes for the first Harry Potter book. She decided to live in Edinburgh to be near her sister. She wrote *Harry Potter and the*

Philosopher's Stone in a café with her three-month-old baby asleep next to her. 'It was cold and miserable in the flat so I went to the café to write,' Rowling says, 'It was the lowest point of my life.' Rowling didn't have much money and she decided to finish the book in one year, then earn some money as a teacher.

Rowling didn't actually need to worry about money. The story of Harry Potter, his magical talents, and his friends and enemies at Hogwarts School was a brilliant success. You can buy the books in 200 different countries. They are the most successful children's books ever with 200 million copies so far around the world. And Joanne Kathleen Rowling is one of the richest women in Britain.

1 Who is J K Rowling?

2 Where was she when she got the idea for Harry Potter?

3 Why didn't she start working on the book seriously in 1990?

4 When did she go to live in Portugal?

5 How did Rowling earn money in Portugal?

6 What did Rowling bring back with her from Portugal?

7 Why did she decide to live in Edinburgh?

8 Where did she write when she was in Edinburgh?

9 Who did she take with her?

10 Why didn't she stay in her flat to write?

11 What are your favourite books?

12 Do you prefer books or films? Why?

Answers

1 ....
2 ....
3 ....
....
4 ....
5 ....
....
6 ....
....
7 ....
....
8 ....
9 ....
10 ....
....
11 ....
....
12 ....
....

2 **Match the signs (A – H) to the meanings (1 – 5). There are two extra signs.**

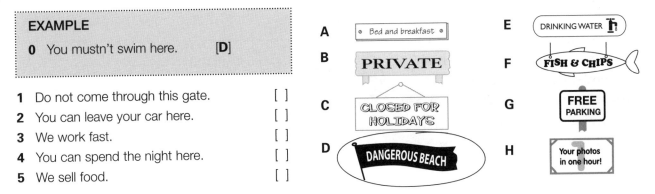

EXAMPLE	
0 You mustn't swim here.	**[D]**

1 Do not come through this gate. [ ]
2 You can leave your car here. [ ]
3 We work fast. [ ]
4 You can spend the night here. [ ]
5 We sell food. [ ]

A ◦ Bed and breakfast ◦
B **PRIVATE**
C CLOSED FOR HOLIDAYS
D DANGEROUS BEACH
E DRINKING WATER
F FISH & CHIPS
G FREE PARKING
H Your photos in one hour!

3 **Complete the article about Elvis Presley with the correct words. Circle A, B or C for each space.**

Elvis Presley wanted **0** bicycle for his eleventh birthday. His mother didn't **1** enough money so she bought him a guitar for just twelve dollars. **2** guitar helped Elvis Presley to become one of **3** famous singers in **4** world.

At the beginning of High School, Elvis was shy and **5** make friends easily. But **6** fifteen he changed. He **7** tight jeans and had long hair. The girls started to like **8**. When he was seventeen he sang **9** the school concert. The whole class heard **10** voice and they loved it. After the concert, Elvis **11** one of the most popular students in the school.

Elvis **12** school at eighteen and got a job as a driver. One day, he **13** a sign, *Record your own song at Sun Studios for $4*. Elvis recorded a song for his **14** birthday. The song was *That's Alright Mama*. A **15** days later they played it on Memphis radio. And the rest is history.

EXAMPLE		
0 **A** some	**B a**	**C** the

	A	B	C
1	**A** got	**B** have	**C** had
2	**A** Those	**B** Them	**C** That
3	**A** the more	**B** the most	**C** most
4	**A** a	**B** every	**C** the
5	**A** didn't	**B** doesn't	**C** can't
6	**A** in	**B** on	**C** at
7	**A** wearing	**B** wear	**C** wore
8	**A** his	**B** him	**C** her
9	**A** in	**B** near	**C** on
10	**A** his	**B** him	**C** her
11	**A** was	**B** did	**C** is
12	**A** stop	**B** left	**C** leave
13	**A** saw	**B** see	**C** seeing
14	**A** mother	**B** mothers	**C** mother's
15	**A** lot	**B** few	**C** little

10

Portfolio Dossier

Write a letter or e-mail telling a friend about a trip you went on recently. Describe some of the places you visited. Write between 70 and 80 words.

Read the *Tips for the task* before you start writing.

Tips for the task

- Start your letter or e-mail in the appropriate way, e.g. *Dear ...* (for a letter) *Hello .... / Hi ....* (for an e-mail).

- With a letter, you will have to write an address and the date. The usual way of writing a date is, e.g. *12th March 200...*

- Only write a very short introduction to the task, e.g. *I had a great time last week. / My parents took me on an amazing trip this summer.* Make sure you say when you went on the trip in this first sentence.

- Then say where you went.

- Don't mention how you travelled and where you stayed. The task is to describe some of the places you visited. You can only write 80 words altogether so you mustn't waste them.

- Describe some of the places you visited. You should describe three. You will need to write three or four sentences about each place. A good way to describe things is to imagine that the other person has no idea about them. For example: *We went to the Colosseum in the afternoon. It's a big Roman amphitheatre. It's nearly 2,000 years old. In Roman times gladiators fought lions there.*

- End your letter like this: *Write and tell me about your trip to ... / I'd really like to hear about your trip to ... Write to me soon. Love/Best wishes from ...*

- When you count your words, don't include the address and date. Make sure you have no less than 70 words and no more than 80.

Write your first draft here.

....

....

....

....

....

....

....

....

....

....

....

....

....

....

....

....

....

....

....

....

....

....

....

....

....

....

....

....

- **When you finish your first draft, show it to your teacher, She/He will give you feedback by filling in the form *Advice to the student*.**

- **Your teacher's feedback will help you to improve your first draft.**

- **When you have improved your first draft with the help of the feedback form, write your final version.**

Student portfolio feedback form

Student's name ....

Task ....

Teacher's signature .... **Date** ....

Advice to the student

- [ ] Your first draft is completely wrong. Start again.
- [ ] You have not done all of the task. Check the instructions again.
- [ ] Your work needs to be tidier.
- [ ] You should add some more ideas.
- [ ] You should add an introduction.
- [ ] You should add a conclusion.
- [ ] You should describe in more detail.
- [ ] You should give more opinions.
- [ ] You should use more varied language.
- [ ] You shouldn't repeat yourself.
- [ ] You should check your spelling.
- [ ] You should check your punctuation.
- [ ] You need to check your verbs.
- [ ] You need to check the grammar.
- [ ] Your handwriting needs to improve.
- [ ] The style of your language is wrong for this task.

Other comments

....

....

....

....

....

Vocabulary builder

The Vocabulary builder gives you all the words in this book in alphabetical order. There is also a space for you to write the translation. Each time you learn a new word, write it in your language. In this way you can create your own dictionary.

English	Phonetic	Translation
A		
about	/əˈbaʊt/	
about ▶ What about …?	/əˈbaʊt/ /wɒt əˈbaʊt…/	
accent	/ˈæksənt/	
across	/əˈkrɒs/	
active	/ˈæktɪv/	
activity	/ækˈtɪvɪti/	
actor	/ˈæktə(r)/	
addition ▶ in addition to	/əˈdɪʃn/ /ɪn əˈdɪʃn tə/	
advert/advertisement	/ˈædvɜːt/ /ədˈvɜːtɪsmənt/	
afraid ▶ I'm afraid …	/əˈfreɪd/ /aɪm əˈfreɪd/	
after	/ˈɑːftə(r)/	
afternoon	/ˌɑːftəˈnuːn/	
afterwards	/ˈɑːftəwədz/	
again	/əˈgen/	
against	/əˈgenst/	
agent	/ˈeɪdʒənt/	
ages ▶ for ages	/ˈeɪdʒɪz/ /fə(r) ˈeɪdʒɪz/	
ago	/əˈgəʊ/	
air	/eə(r)/	
airport	/ˈeəpɔːt/	
album	/ˈælbəm/	
all	/ɔːl/	
all over ▶ **It went all over the floor.**	/ɪt went ˌɔːl əʊvə ðə ˈflɔː(r)/	
all right	/ˌɔːl ˈraɪt/	
alone	/əˈləʊn/	
along	/əˈlɒŋ/	
always	/ˈɔːlweɪz/	
ambition	/æmˈbɪʃn/	
ancient	/ˈeɪnʃənt/	
angry	/ˈæŋgri/	
animal	/ˈænɪməl/	
annoying	/əˈnɔɪɪŋ/	
another	/əˈnʌðə(r)/	
answer	/ˈɑːnsə(r)/	
anything, not … anything	/ˈeniθɪŋ/ /nɒt … ˈeniθɪŋ/	
Anyway, …	/ˈeniweɪ/	
apart from	/əˈpɑːt frəm/	
anywhere ▶ I didn't see (her) anywhere	/ˈeniweə(r)/ /aɪ dɪdnt siː hɜː(r) ˈeniweə(r)/	
appear	/əˈpɪə(r)/	
appearance	/əˈpɪərəns/	
apple	/ˈæpl/	
appointment	/əˈpɔɪntmənt/	
area	/ˈeərɪə/	
arm	/ɑːm/	
arrive	/əˈraɪv/	
artist	/ˈɑːtɪst/	

English	Phonetic	Translation
as	/æz, əz/	
asleep	/əˈsliːp/	
ask	/ɑːsk/	
ate ◀ eat	/eɪt, iːt/	
athletics	/æθˈletɪks/	
attention ▶ pay attention	/əˈtenʃn/ /peɪ əˈtenʃn/	
audition	/ɔːˈdɪʃn/	
aunt	/ɑːnt/	
automatically	/ˌɔːtəˈmætɪkli/	
awake	/əˈweɪk/	
B		
back ▶ be back	/bæk/ /bɪ ˈbæk/	
back ▶ have back	/bæk/ /hæv ˈbæk/	
back	/bæk/	
bad	/bæd/	
badge	/bædʒ/	
bag	/bæg/	
bakery	/ˈbeɪkəri/	
banana	/bəˈnɑːnə/	
band	/bænd/	
barbecue	/ˈbɑːbəkjuː/	
bark	/bɑːk/	
basketball	/ˈbɑːskɪtbɔːl/	
bat	/bæt/	
bath	/bɑːθ/	
bathroom	/ˈbɑːθruːm/	
beach	/biːtʃ/	
bean	/biːn/	
beard	/ˈbɪəd/	
beautiful	/ˈbjuːtɪfʊl/	
became ◀ become	/bɪˈkeɪm, bɪˈkʌm/	
because	/bɪˈkʌz/	
become	/bɪˈkʌm/	
bed	/bed/	
bedtime	/ˈbedtaɪm/	
beef	/biːf/	
before	/bɪˈfɔː(r)/	
behind	/bɪˈhaɪnd/	
believe	/bɪˈliːv/	
bell	/bel/	
bench	/bentʃ/	
best friend	/best ˈfrend/	
between	/bɪˈtwiːn/	
big	/bɪg/	
bike	/baɪk/	
bin	/bɪn/	
biography	/baɪˈɒgrəfi/	
birth ▶ date of birth	/bɜːθ, deɪt əv ˈbɜːθ/	

English	Phonetic	Translation
rthday	/ˈbɜːθdeɪ/	
te	/baɪt/	
lack	/blæk/	
londe	/blɒnd/	
lood	/blʌd/	
low	/bləʊ/	
lue	/bluː/	
oard	/bɔːd/	
oat	/bəʊt/	
ook	/bʊk/	
ookshop	/ˈbʊkʃɒp/	
order	/ˈbɔːdə(r)/	
ored	/bɔːd/	
oring	/ˈbɔːrɪŋ/	
orn ► was born	/bɔːn, wəz ˈbɔːn/	
orrow	/ˈbɒrəʊ/	
oth	/bəʊθ/	
ottle	/ˈbɒtl/	
ought ◄ buy	/bɔːt, baɪ/	
ox/basket,	/bɒks, ˈbɑːskɪt/	
icnic box/basket	/ˈpɪknɪk bɒks, bɑːskɪt/	
oy ► boys' school	/bɔɪ/ /bɔɪz skuːl/	
oyfriend	/ˈbɔɪfrend/	
racelet	/ˈbreɪslət/	
read	/bred/	
reak	/breɪk/	
reakfast	/ˈbrekfəst/	
ridge	/brɪdʒ/	
rilliant	/ˈbrɪliənt/	
Britain	/ˈbrɪtən/	
rought back ◄ bring back	/brɔːt bæk, brɪŋ bæk/	
rown	/braʊn/	
rush ► brush teeth	/brʌʃ/ /brʌʃ ˈtiːθ/	
building	/ˈbɪldɪŋ/	
built ◄ build	/bɪlt/ /bɪld/	
burn	/bɜːn/	
burnt ◄ burn	/bɜːnt, bɜːn/	
bus	/bʌs/	
bus stop	/ˈbʌs stɒp/	
busy	/ˈbɪzɪ/	
but	/bʌt/	
butcher's	/ˈbʊtʃəz/	
butter	/ˈbʌtə(r)/	
buy	/baɪ/	
by, by 5.30	/baɪ, baɪ faɪv ˈθɜːtɪ/	

C

English	Phonetic	Translation
cackle	/ˈkækl/	
café	/ˈkæfeɪ/	
cake	/keɪk/	
call	/kɔːl/	
came ◄ come	/keɪm, kʌm/	
camera	/ˈkæmrə/	

English	Phonetic	Translation
camp	/kæmp/	
camping, go camping	/ˈkæmpɪŋ, gəʊ ˈkæmpɪŋ/	
campsite	/ˈkæmpsaɪt/	
can	/kæn/	
Can I help you?	/kən aɪ ˈhelp juː/	
Can I take a message?	/kən aɪ ˌteɪk ə ˈmesɪdʒ/	
canoeing	/kəˈnuːɪŋ/	
capital	/ˈkæpɪtl/	
car	/kɑː(r)/	
car park	/ˈkɑː pɑːk/	
card	/kɑːd/	
careful ► Be careful!	/ˈkeəfʊl, bɪ ˈkeəfʊl/	
carefully	/ˈkeəfʊlɪ/	
carnival	/ˈkɑːnɪvəl/	
Caribbean	/ˌkærɪˈbiːən/	
carrot	/ˈkærət/	
carry	/ˈkærɪ/	
cartoon	/kɑːˈtuːn/	
cat	/kæt/	
catch	/kætʃ/	
cathedral	/kəˈθiːdrəl/	
cave	/keɪv/	
CD player	/siː ˈdiː pleɪə(r)/	
celebrate	/ˈseləbreɪt/	
celebration	/ˌseləˈbreɪʃn/	
cell phone (*American English*)	/ˈsel fəʊn/	
cereal	/ˈsɪərɪəl/	
champion	/ˈtʃæmpɪən/	
championship	/ˈtʃæmpɪənʃɪp/	
chance ► no chance	/tʃɑːns/ /ˈnəʊ tʃɑːns/	
character	/ˈkærɪktə(r)/	
charity	/ˈtʃærɪtɪ/	
chat up	/tʃæt ˈʌp/	
check	/tʃek/	
cheek	/tʃiːk/	
cheese	/tʃiːz/	
cheese shop	/ˈtʃiːz ʃɒp/	
chemist's	/ˈkemɪsts/	
chewing gum	/ˈtʃuːɪŋ gʌm/	
chicken	/ˈtʃɪkn/	
children	/ˈtʃɪldrən/	
chin	/tʃɪn/	
Chinese	/tʃaɪˈniːz/	
chocolate	/ˈtʃɒklət/	
choose	/tʃuːz/	
church, the Catholic Church	/tʃɜːtʃ/ /ðə ˈkæθlɪk tʃɜːtʃ/	
cinema	/ˈsɪnəmə/	
circus	/ˈsɜːkəs/	
city	/ˈsɪtɪ/	
clap	/klæp/	
class	/klɑːs/	
classroom	/ˈklɑːsruːm/	

English	Phonetic	Translation
clean	/kli:n/	
clever	/'klevə(r)/	
click	/klɪk/	
climb	/klaɪm/	
close	/kləʊz/	
clothes shop	/'kləʊðz ʃɒp/	
cloud	/klaʊd/	
cloudy	/'klaʊdɪ/	
club	/klʌb/	
coaching	/'kəʊtʃɪŋ/	
coast	/kəʊst/	
coffee	/'kɒfɪ/	
cold ▶ It's cold.	/kəʊld/ /ɪts 'kəʊld/	
collect	/kə'lekt/	
college	/'kɒlɪdʒ/	
comb	/kəʊm/	
come	/kʌm/	
come in	/kʌm 'ɪn/	
comedy programme	/'kɒmədɪ prəʊɡræm/	
compass	/'kʌmpəs/	
compass point	/'kʌmpəs pɔɪnt/	
compete	/kəm'pi:t/	
competition	/kɒmpə'tɪʃn/	
computer	/kəm'pju:tə(r)/	
concert	/'kɒnsət/	
Congratulations!	/kənɡrætʃʊ'leɪʃnz/	
cook	/kʊk/	
cookie (*American English*)	/'kʊkɪ/	
cost	/kɒst/	
Could you say ... phoned?	/'kʊd ju: seɪ ... ˌfəʊnd/	
Could you tell me the way to ...?	/'kʊd ju: tel mi: ðə weɪ tə.../	
course ▶ of course	/kɔ:s/ /əv 'kɔ:s/	
court	/kɔ:t/	
cousin	/'kʌzn/	
covers (of a bed)	/'kʌvəz/	
crash into	/kræʃ 'ɪntə/	
cricket	/'krɪkɪt/	
crisps	/krɪsps/	
cropped	/krɒpt/	
cross	/krɒs/	
cuddle	/'kʌdl/	
cupboard	/'kʌbəd/	
curly	/'kɜ:lɪ/	
currency	/'kʌrənsɪ/	
cycle	/'saɪkl/	

D

English	Phonetic	Translation
dance	/dɑ:ns/	
dangerous	/'deɪndʒərəs/	
dark skinned	/dɑ:k skɪnd/	
dark, dark brown	/dɑ:k, dɑ:k 'braʊn/	
dark, after dark	/dɑ:k, ɑftə 'dɑ:k/	

English	Phonetic	Translation
daughter	/'dɔ:tə(r)/	
day out	/deɪ 'aʊt/	
dear ▶ Oh dear!	/dɪə(r)/ /əʊ 'dɪə(r)/	
decide	/dɪ'saɪd/	
deep	/di:p/	
delicatessen	/delɪkə'tesn/	
deliver	/dɪ'lɪvə(r)/	
dentist's	/'dentɪsts/	
department store	/dɪ'pɑ:tmənt stɔ:(r)/	
desert (n)	/'dezət/	
designer	/dɪ'zaɪnə(r)/	
desk	/desk/	
detention	/dɪ'tenʃn/	
devil	/'devl/	
diary	/'daɪərɪ/	
did ◄ do	/dɪd, du:/	
different	/'dɪfrənt/	
difficult	/'dɪfɪkəlt/	
dinnertime	/'dɪnətaɪm/	
discover	/dɪs'kʌvə(r)/	
discoverer	/dɪs'kʌvərə(r)/	
discovery	/dɪs'kʌvərɪ/	
display	/dɪs'pleɪ/	
distance	/'dɪstəns/	
district	/'dɪstrɪkt/	
divorce	/dɪ'vɔ:s/	
do well	/du: 'wel/	
doctor	/'dɒktə(r)/	
documentary	/dɒkjʊ'mentrɪ/	
doll	/dɒl/	
done ▶ Well done!	/dʌn/ /wel 'dʌn/	
donkey	/'dɒŋkɪ/	
door	/dɔ:(r)/	
doorway	/'dɔ:weɪ/	
doughnut	/'dəʊnʌt/	
down	/daʊn/	
dragon	/'dræɡən/	
dress	/dres/	
dress up	/dres 'ʌp/	
drink	/drɪŋk/	
drive	/draɪv/	
drop	/drɒp/	
drums	/drʌmz/	
dry	/draɪ/	
dune	/dju:n/	
during	/'dʒʊərɪŋ/	

E

English	Phonetic	Translation
each other	/i:tʃ 'ʌðə(r)/	
ear	/ɪə(r)/	
early	/'ɜ:lɪ/	
earn	/ɜ:n/	

English	Phonetic	Translation
earring	/ˈɪərɪŋ/	
earth	/ɜːθ/	
easily	/ˈiːzɪlɪ/	
east	/iːst/	
Easter	/ˈiːstə(r)/	
easy	/ˈiːzɪ/	
eat	/iːt/	
ecology	/ɪˈkɒlədʒɪ/	
education	/edʒʊˈkeɪʃn/	
effects, special effects	/ɪˈfekts, speʃl ɪˈfekts/	
egg	/eg/	
either ... or	/ˈaɪðə(r) ... ɔː(r)/	
elegant	/ˈelɪgənt/	
else ? **What else?**	/els/ /wɒt ˈels/	
e-mail	/ˈiː meɪl/	
emperor	/ˈempərə(r)/	
end ▶ in the end	/end/ /ɪn ðiː ˈend/	
enemy	/ˈenəmɪ/	
energetic	/enəˈdʒetɪk/	
energy	/ˈenədʒɪ/	
enjoy	/ɪnˈdʒɔɪ/	
enough	/ɪˈnʌf/	
enough ▶ **That's enough.**	/ɪˈnʌf/ /ðæts ɪˈnʌf/	
episode	/ˈepɪsəʊd/	
erupt	/ɪˈrʌpt/	
establish	/ɪˈstæblɪʃ/	
even	/ˈiːvn/	
evening	/ˈiːvnɪŋ/	
ever ▶ the first ever	/ˈevə(r)/ /ðə fɜːst ˈevə(r)/	
every	/ˈevrɪ/	
everybody	/ˈevrɪbɒdɪ/	
everything	/ˈevrɪθɪŋ/	
exactly	/ɪkˈzæktlɪ/	
exam	/ɪkˈzæm/	
excellent	/ˈeksələnt/	
Excuse me.	/ɪkˈskjuːz mɪ/	
exhausted	/ɪkˈzɔːstɪd/	
exotic	/ɪkˈzɒtɪk/	
expect ▶ I didn't expect to get a place	/ɪkˈspekt/ /aɪ dɪdnt ɪkˈspekt tə get ə pleɪs/	
expensive	/ɪkˈspensɪv/	
eye	/aɪ/	
eyebrows	/ˈaɪbraʊz/	

F

English	Phonetic	Translation
face	/feɪs/	
fair skinned	/feə(r) skɪnd/	
fall	/fɔːl/	
fall off	/fɔːl ˈɒf/	
famous	/ˈfeɪməs/	
fantastic	/fænˈtæstɪk/	
fast	/fɑːst/	

English	Phonetic	Translation
favourite	/ˈfeɪvərɪt/	
feel	/fiːl/	
feet	/fiːt/	
fell ◀ fall	/fel, fɔːl/	
few	/fjuː/	
field	/fiːld/	
film	/fɪlm/	
find	/faɪnd/	
finger	/ˈfɪŋgə(r)/	
finish	/ˈfɪnɪʃ/	
finish time	/ˈfɪnɪʃ taɪm/	
fire	/ˈfaɪə(r)/	
fireworks	/ˈfaɪəwɜːks/	
first	/fɜːst/	
fish	/fɪʃ/	
fishmonger	/ˈfɪʃmʌŋgə(r)/	
fitness training	/ˈfɪtnəs treɪnɪŋ/	
fizzy ▶ fizzy drink	/ˈfɪzɪ/ /ˈfɪzɪ ˈdrɪŋk/	
flat	/flæt/	
fleece	/fliːs/	
flew ◀ fly	/fluː, flaɪ/	
floor	/flɔː(r)/	
flour	/ˈflaʊə(r)/	
fly	/flaɪ/	
foggy ▶ It's foggy.	/ˈfɒgɪ/ /ɪts ˈfɒgɪ/	
follow	/ˈfɒləʊ /	
food	/fuːd/	
foot	/fʊt/	
football	/ˈfʊtbɔːl/	
forehead	/ˈfɔːhed/	
forest	/ˈfɒrɪst/	
forget	/fəˈget/	
Formula One	/fɔːmjʊlə ˈwʌn/	
forward ▶ look forward to	/ˈfɔːwəd/ /lʊk ˈfɔːwəd tə/	
found ◀ find	/faʊnd, faɪnd/	
freckles	/ˈfreklz/	
free time	/friː ˈtaɪm/	
French fries (*American English*)	/frentʃ ˈfraɪz/	
fridge	/frɪdʒ/	
friend	/frend/	
friendly	/ˈfrendlɪ/	
frightened ▶ I'm frightened of...	/ˈfraɪtənd/ /aɪm ˈfraɪtənd əv.../	
fringe	/frɪndʒ/	
frozen	/ˈfrəʊzn/	
fruit	/fruːt/	
fruit and vegetable shop	/fruːt ən ˈvedʒtəbl ʃɒp/	
fun	/fʌn/	
funny	/ˈfʌnɪ/	
fussy	/ˈfʌsɪ/	

English	Phonetic	Translation
G		
game	/geɪm/	
garden	/ˈgɑːdn/	
gate	/geɪt/	
gave ◄ give	/geɪv, gɪv/	
generous	/ˈdʒenərəs/	
Geography	/dʒɒgrəfɪ/	
get ► he gets £10	/get/ /hiː gets ten ˈpaʊndz/	
get dressed	/get ˈdrest/	
get off	/get ˈɒf/	
get up	/get ˈʌp/	
ghost	/gəʊst/	
girl ► girls' school	/gɜːl/ /gɜːlz skuːl/	
give	/gɪv/	
gladiator	/ˈglædieɪtə(r)/	
glass	/glɑːs/	
glasses	/ˈglɑːsɪz/	
go	/gəʊ/	
go in for	/gəʊ ˈɪn fə(r)/	
goalkeeper	/ˈgəʊlkiːpə(r)/	
god	/gɒd/	
Golden Jubilee	/ˈgəʊldn dʒuːbɪˈliː/	
good	/gʊd/	
good ► be good at	/gʊd/ /bɪ ˈgʊd ət/	
government	/ˈgʌvənmənt/	
grade ► A grade	/greɪd/ /ˈeɪ greɪd/	
grandfather	/ˈgrænfɑːðə(r)/	
grandmother	/ˈgrænmʌðə(r)/	
grandparents	/ˈgrænpeərənts/	
grandson	/ˈgrændsʌn/	
grape	/greɪp/	
great	/greɪt/	
green	/griːn/	
grey	/greɪ/	
Guess what?	/ges ˈwɒt/	
Guides	/gaɪdz/	
guitar	/gɪˈtɑː(r)/	
H		
had ◄ have	/hæd, hæv/	
hair	/heə(r)/	
hairdresser's	/ˈheədresəz/	
hairstyle	/ˈheəstaɪl/	
Hallowe'en	/hæləʊˈiːn/	
ham	/hæm/	
hand	/hænd/	
Hands off!	/hændz ˈɒf/	
Hang on a minute!	/ˌhæŋ ˈɒn ə mɪnɪt/	
happen	/ˈhæpn/	
happy ► He wasn't happy.	/ˈhæpɪ/ /hiː wɒznt ˈhæpɪ/	
hard	/hɑːd/	
hat	/hæt/	
head	/hed/	

English	Phonetic	Translation
head of state	/hed əv ˈsteɪt/	
health	/helθ/	
heard ◄ hear	/hɜːd, hɪə(r)/	
heavy	/ˈhevɪ/	
hell	/hel/	
Hello, could I speak to ..., please?	/heˈləʊ, kʊd aɪ spiːk tə ... pliːz/	
help	/help/	
help yourself	/help jɔːˈself/	
helpful	/ˈhelpfʊl/	
Here's your change.	/hɪəz jɔː ˈtʃeɪndʒ/	
hide	/haɪd/	
high	/haɪ/	
hit ◄ hit	/hɪt, hɪt/	
hobby	/ˈhɒbɪ/	
hold onto	/həʊld ˈɒntə/	
holiday	/ˈhɒlɪdeɪ/	
home	/həʊm/	
homework	/ˈhəʊmwɜːk/	
hoot	/huːt/	
hospital	/ˈhɒspɪtl/	
hot ► It's hot.	/hɒt/ /ɪts ˈhɒt/	
hour	/ˈaʊə(r)/	
house	/haʊs/	
How much is ... ?	/haʊ ˈmʌtʃ ɪz.../	
How's the pizza?	/ˌhaʊz ðə ˈpiːtsə/	
howl	/haʊl/	
huge	/hjuːdʒ/	
hundred	/ˈhʌndrəd/	
hungry ► be hungry	/ˈhʌŋgrɪ/ /bɪ ˈhʌŋgrɪ/	
hurry	/ˈhʌrɪ/	
hurt yourself	/hɜːt jɔːˈself/	
I		
I don't care.	/aɪ dəʊnt ˈkeə(r)/	
I don't know.	/aɪ dəʊnt ˈnəʊ/	
I don't think so.	/aɪ dəʊnt ˈθɪŋk səʊ/	
I know.	/aɪ ˈnəʊ/	
I think so too.	/aɪ θɪŋk səʊ ˈtuː/	
I want to ...	/aɪ wɒnt tə.../	
I was only joking.	/aɪ wəz ˌəʊnlɪ ˈdʒəʊkɪŋ/	
I'd like ... please.	/aɪd laɪk ...ˌpliːz/	
I'll just watch.	/aɪl dʒʌst ˈwɒtʃ/	
I'm sorry, he isn't here.	/aɪm ˌsɒrɪ, hiː ɪznt ˈhɪə(r)/	
ice cream	/ˈaɪs kriːm/	
ice hockey	/ˈaɪs hɒkɪ/	
ice skating	/ˈaɪs skeɪtɪŋ/	
idea ► Great idea!	/aɪˈdɪə/ /ˈgreɪt aɪˌdɪə/	
ill	/ɪl/	
imagine	/ɪˈmædʒɪn/	
independence	/ɪndəˈpendəns/	
industrial	/ɪnˈdʌstrɪəl/	
inside	/ɪnˈsaɪd/	

English	Phonetic	Translation
instrument	/ˈɪnstrəmənt/	
interest	/ˈɪntrest/	
interesting	/ˈɪntrəstɪŋ/	
international	/ˌɪntəˈnæʃnl/	
internet ▶ surf the internet	/ˈɪntənet/ /sɜːf ði: ˈɪntənet/	
into	/ˈɪntə/	
invite	/ɪnˈvaɪt/	
Is it far?	/ɪz ɪt ˈfɑː(r)/	
island	/ˈaɪlənd/	
It's about a dog and a wizard.	/ɪts əbaʊt ə ˌdɒg ənd ə ˈwɪzəd/	
It's fun.	/ɪts ˈfʌn/	
It's lovely.	/ɪts ˈlʌvlɪ/	
It's not fair.	/ɪts nɒt ˈfeə(r)/	
It's not far.	/ɪts nɒt ˈfɑː(r)/	
It's only a toy spider.	/ɪts ˌəʊnlɪ ə ˌtɔɪ ˈspaɪdə(r)/	
It's quite a long way.	/ɪts ˌkwaɪt ə lɒŋ ˈweɪ/	
It's time for bed.	/ɪts ˌtaɪm fə ˈbed/	
J		
jacket	/ˈdʒækɪt/	
Japanese	/dʒæpəˈniːz/	
jeans	/dʒiːnz/	
jewel	/ˈdʒʊəl/	
jeweller's	/ˈdʒʊələz/	
job	/dʒɒb/	
join	/dʒɔɪn/	
journey	/ˈdʒɜːnɪ/	
juice	/dʒuːs/	
jump	/dʒʌmp/	
jumper	/ˈdʒʌmpə(r)/	
jungle	/ˈdʒʌŋgl/	
junior	/ˈdʒuːnɪə(r)/	
just	/dʒʌst/	
Just then	/dʒʌst ˈðen/	
K		
karate	/kəˈrɑːtɪ/	
kart	/kɑːt/	
karting, go karting	/ˈkɑːtɪŋ, gəʊ ˈkɑːtɪŋ/	
keep	/kiːp/	
keep away	/kiːp əˈweɪ/	
key ring	/ˈkiːrɪŋ/	
kind	/kaɪnd/	
king	/kɪŋ/	
kit, sports kit	/kɪt, spɔːts kɪt/	
kitchen	/ˈkɪtʃɪn/	
kite	/kaɪt/	
knee	/niː/	
knock	/nɒk/	
knock into	/nɒk ˈɪntə/	
know ▶ you know	/nəʊ/ /ju: ˈnəʊ/	

English	Phonetic	Translation
L		
lake	/leɪk/	
lamb	/læm/	
land	/lænd/	
language	/ˈlæŋgwɪdʒ/	
large	/lɑːdʒ/	
last ▶ When did you last ...?	/lɑːst/ /ˌwen dɪd ju: lɑːst.../	
last night	/lɑːst ˈnaɪt/	
late	/leɪt/	
laugh	/lɑːf/	
learn	/lɜːn/	
leave	/liːv/	
leave on	/liːv ˈɒn/	
left	/left/	
left ◀ leave	/left, liːv/	
left ▶ Is there much left?	/left/ /ɪz ðeə mʌtʃ ˈleft/	
leg	/leg/	
lemon	/ˈlemən/	
let	/let/	
Let's ...	/lets.../	
letter	/ˈletə(r)/	
licence ▶ driving licence	/ˈlaɪsəns/ /ˈdraɪvɪŋ laɪsəns/	
lie	/laɪ/	
life	/laɪf/	
lift ▶ offer a lift	/lɪft/ /ˈɒfə(r) ə ˈlɪft/	
light	/laɪt/	
light ▶ light brown	/laɪt/ /laɪt ˈbraʊn/	
lightning	/ˈlaɪtnɪŋ/	
like	/laɪk/	
like ▶ What ... like?	/laɪk/ /wɒt ... ˈlaɪk/	
lip	/lɪp/	
lipstick	/ˈlɪpstɪk/	
listen to	/ˈlɪsn tə/	
litter	/ˈlɪtə(r)/	
litter bin	/ˈlɪtə bɪn/	
little	/ˈlɪtl/	
little ▶ a little	/ˈlɪtl/ /ə ˈlɪtl/	
living room	/ˈlɪvɪŋ ruːm/	
local	/ˈləʊkl/	
long	/lɒŋ/	
long ▶ for long	/lɒŋ/ /fə ˈlɒŋ/	
long ▶ How long ...?	/lɒŋ/ /haʊ ˈlɒŋ/	
long ▶ I won't be long.	/lɒŋ/ /aɪ wəʊnt bɪ ˈlɒŋ/	
look after	/lʊk ˈɑːftə(r)/	
look at	/ˈlʊk ət/	
look forward ▶ I'm looking forward to...	/lʊk ˈfɔːwəd/ /aɪm ˈlʊkɪŋ fɔːwəd tə.../	
lose	/luːz/	
lost ▶ get lost	/lɒst, get lɒst/	
lot ▶ a lot of	/lɒt, ə lɒt əv/	
lots of	/ˈlɒts əv/	
loud	/laʊd/	

English	Phonetic	Translation
love	/lʌv/	
lovely	/ˈlʌvlɪ/	
low	/ləʊ/	
loyal	/ˈlɔɪəl/	
luck	/lʌk/	
lunch	/lʌntʃ/	
lunchtime	/ˈlʌntʃtaɪm/	

M

English	Phonetic	Translation
made ◄ make	/meɪd, meɪk/	
magazine	/ˌmægəˈziːn/	
magic	/ˈmædʒɪk/	
mall (American English)	/mɔːl/	
map	/mæp/	
mark	/mɑːk/	
market	/ˈmɑːkɪt/	
marry	/ˈmærɪ/	
match ► football match	/mætʃ/ /ˈfʊtbɔːl mætʃ/	
maze	/meɪz/	
meal	/miːl/	
meaning	/ˈmiːnɪŋ/	
meat	/miːt/	
medium ► of medium height	/ˈmiːdɪəm/ /əv ˈmiːdɪəm haɪt/	
medium length	/ˈmiːdɪəm leŋθ/	
meet	/miːt/	
melon	/ˈmelən/	
member	/ˈmembə(r)/	
mermaid	/ˈmɜːmeɪd/	
mess	/mes/	
microwave	/ˈmaɪkrəʊweɪv/	
middle	/ˈmɪdl/	
midnight	/ˈmɪdnaɪt/	
mile ► for miles	/maɪl/ /fə ˈmaɪlz/	
milk	/mɪlk/	
mind ► Never mind.	/maɪnd/ /nevə maɪnd/	
mine	/maɪn/	
minute	/ˈmɪnɪt/	
miss	/mɪs/	
moan	/məʊn/	
mobile phone	/məʊbaɪl ˈfəʊn/	
model	/ˈmɒdl/	
mole	/məʊl/	
moment ► at the moment	/ˈməʊmənt / /ət ðə ˈməʊmənt/	
monarchy	/ˈmɒnəkɪ/	
money	/ˈmʌnɪ/	
monster	/ˈmɒnstə(r)/	
month	/mʌnθ/	
monument	/ˈmɒnjʊmənt/	
mood	/muːd/	
moon	/muːn/	
morning	/ˈmɔːnɪŋ/	

English	Phonetic	Translation
most	/məʊst/	
motor racing	/ˈməʊtə reɪsɪŋ/	
mountain	/ˈmaʊntɪn/	
mountain range	/ˈmaʊntɪn reɪndʒ/	
moustache	/mʊsˈtɑːʃ/	
mouth	/maʊθ/	
movie theater (American English)	/ˈmuːvɪ θɪətə(r)/	
museum	/mjuːˈzɪəm/	
mushroom	/ˈmʌʃrʊm/	
music	/ˈmjuːzɪk/	
music programme	/ˈmjuːzɪk prəʊgræm/	
music store	/ˈmjuːzɪk stɔː(r)/	
musician	/mjuːˈzɪʃn/	
must	/mʌst/	

N

English	Phonetic	Translation
nail	/neɪl/	
nature programme	/ˈneɪtʃə prəʊgræm/	
naughty	/ˈnɔːtɪ/	
near	/nɪə(r)/	
nearly	/ˈnɪəlɪ/	
neat ► That's neat.	/niːt/ /ðæts ˈniːt/	
neck	/nek/	
necklace	/ˈnekləs/	
need	/niːd/	
never	/ˈnevə(r)/	
new	/njuː/	
New Year	/njuː ˈjɪə(r)/	
news	/njuːz/	
news ► the news	/njuːz/ /ðə ˈnjuːz/	
newsagent's	/ˈnjuːzeɪdʒənts/	
newspaper	/ˈnjuːspeɪpə(r)/	
next	/nekst/	
nice	/naɪs/	
nobody	/ˈnəʊbɒdɪ/	
noise	/nɔɪz/	
north	/nɔːθ/	
north-east	/nɔːθ ˈiːst/	
north-west	/nɔːθ ˈwest/	
nose	/nəʊz/	
Not for me.	/nɒt fə ˈmiː/	
nothing	/ˈnʌθɪŋ/	
notice	/ˈnəʊtɪs/	
now	/naʊ/	

O

English	Phonetic	Translation
observatory	/əbˈzɜːvətrɪ/	
ocean	/ˈəʊʃn/	
off ► have a day off	/ɒf/ /hæv ə deɪ ˈɒf/	
offer	/ˈɒfə(r)/	
often	/ˈɒfn/	
often ► more often	/ˈɒfn/ /mɔː(r) ˈɒfn/	

English	Phonetic	Translation
h, I see.	/əʊ aɪ 'siː/	
l	/ɔɪl/	
l lamp	/ɔɪl læmp/	
nk, oink!	/'ɔɪŋk, ɔɪŋk/	
K	/əʊ 'keɪ/	
ld	/əʊld/	
ld-fashioned	/əʊld 'fæʃnd/	
lympic Games	/ə.lɪmpɪk 'ɡeɪmz/	
n ▶ be on	/ɒn/ /biː ɒn/	
ne	/wʌn/	
nion	/'ʌnjən/	
nly	/'əʊnlɪ/	
Oops!	/ʊps/	
pen	/'əʊpn/	
pen top bus	/əʊpn tɒp 'bʌs/	
range	/'ɒrɪndʒ/	
rganisation	/ɔːɡənaɪ'zeɪʃn/	
ther	/ʌðə(r)/	
ut ▶ be out	/aʊt/ /biː 'aʊt/	
utdoor	/'aʊtdɔː(r)/	
utside	/aʊt'saɪd/	
ver	/'əʊvə(r)/	
wl	/aʊl/	
wn ▶ on your own	/əʊn/ /ɒn jə(r) 'əʊn/	

P

English	Phonetic	Translation
ack one's bags	/pæk wʌnz 'bæɡz/	
ain	/peɪn/	
alace	/'pælɪs/	
ale	/peɪl/	
ancake	/'pænkeɪk/	
anther	/'pænθə(r)/	
aper	/'peɪpə(r)/	
aper round, do a paper round	/'peɪpə raʊnd, duː ə 'peɪpə raʊnd/	
arade	/pə'reɪd/	
arent	/'peərənt/	
ark the car	/pɑːk ðə kɑː(r)/	
art	/pɑːt/	
art ▶ take part in	/pɑːt/ /teɪk 'pɑːt ɪn/	
arty	/'pɑːtɪ/	
artying	/'pɑːtɪɪŋ/	
ass	/pɑːs/	
ast	/pɑːst/	
ath	/pɑːθ/	
atient	/'peɪʃənt/	
ay for	/'peɪ fə(r)/	
ea	/piː/	
encil case	/'pensɪl keɪs/	
en-friend	/'penfrend/	
eople ▶ people say	/'piːpl/ /'piːpl 'seɪ/	
epper	/'pepə(r)/	
erform	/pə'fɔːm/	

English	Phonetic	Translation
perhaps	/pə'hæps/	
person	/'pɜːsən/	
personal CD player	/'pɜːsənl siː 'diː pleɪə(r)/	
personality	/pɜːsə'nælɪtɪ/	
pet	/pet/	
pharmacy (American English)	/'fɑːməsɪ/	
phone	/fəʊn/	
photo	/'fəʊtəʊ/	
piano lesson	/pɪ'ænəʊ lesn/	
pick up	/pɪk 'ʌp/	
picnic	/'pɪknɪk/	
picture	/'pɪktʃə(r)/	
piece	/piːs/	
pig	/pɪɡ/	
pink	/pɪŋk/	
place	/pleɪs/	
plan	/plæn/	
plant	/plɑːnt/	
play	/pleɪ/	
play ▶ school play	/pleɪ/ /skuːl 'pleɪ/	
player	/'pleɪə(r)/	
please	/pliːz/	
plenty of	/'plentɪ əv/	
pocket money	/'pɒkɪt mʌnɪ/	
poetry	/'pəʊətrɪ/	
point your toes	/'pɔɪnt jə 'təʊz/	
pointed	/'pɔɪntɪd/	
pool	/puːl/	
popular	/'pɒpjʊlə(r)/	
population	/pɒpjʊ'leɪʃn/	
port	/pɔːt/	
post	/pəʊst/	
postcard	/'pəʊskɑːd/	
potato	/pə'teɪtəʊ/	
potato chips (American English)	/pəteɪtəʊ 'tʃɪps/	
pounds	/paʊndz/	
practical	/'præktɪkl/	
practise	/'præktɪs/	
present	/'preznt/	
prison	/'prɪzn/	
prize	/praɪz/	
probably	/'prɒbəblɪ/	
professional	/prə'feʃnl/	
programme	/'prəʊɡræm/	
project	/'prɒdʒekt/	
protect	/prə'tekt/	
Protestant	/'prɒtɪstənt/	
proud of	/praʊd əv/	
pudding ▶ Christmas pudding	/'pʊdɪŋ/ /krɪsməs 'pʊdɪŋ/	
pull out of	/pʊl 'aʊt əv/	
purple	/'pɜːpl/	

English	Phonetic	Translation
purpose ▶	/ˈpɜːpəs/	
You did that on purpose.	/juː ˌdɪd ðæt ɒn ˈpɜːpəs/	
purse	/pɜːs/	
push	/pʊʃ/	
put	/pʊt/	
put back	/pʊt ˈbæk/	
put on	/pʊt ˈɒn/	
put up	/pʊt ˈʌp/	
pyramid	/ˈpɪrəmɪd/	

Q

English	Phonetic	Translation
queen	/kwiːn/	
quick	/kwɪk/	
quickly	/ˈkwɪklɪ/	
quiet	/ˈkwaɪət/	
quietly	/ˈkwaɪətlɪ/	
quite	/kwaɪt/	
quiz show	/ˈkwɪz ʃəʊ/	

R

English	Phonetic	Translation
race (n)	/reɪs/	
race (v)	/reɪs/	
racing driver	/ˈreɪsɪŋ draɪvə(r)/	
rain	/reɪn/	
rainforest	/ˈreɪnfɒrɪst/	
raining ▶ **It's raining.**	/ˈreɪnɪŋ/ /ɪts ˈreɪnɪŋ/	
raise money	/reɪz ˈmʌnɪ/	
read	/riːd/	
ready	/ˈredɪ/	
really	/ˈrɪəlɪ/	
really ▶ not really	/ˈrɪəlɪ/ /nɒt ˈrɪəlɪ/	
reason	/ˈriːzn/	
recently	/ˈriːsəntlɪ/	
record (n)	/ˈrekɔːd/	
record (v)	/rɪˈkɔːd/	
recycle	/riːˈsaɪkl/	
red	/red/	
reddish-brown	/redɪʃ ˈbraʊn/	
reign	/reɪn/	
relax	/rɪˈlæks/	
remember	/rɪˈmembə(r)/	
repeat	/rɪˈpiːt/	
republic	/rɪˈpʌblɪk/	
rice	/raɪs/	
rich	/rɪtʃ/	
ride ▶ bike ride	/raɪd/ /ˈbaɪk raɪd/	
ride one's bike	/raɪd wʌnz ˈbaɪk/	
right	/raɪt/	
ring	/rɪŋ/	
river	/ˈrɪvə(r)/	
road	/rəʊd/	
roller-blading	/ˈrəʊləbleɪdɪŋ/	

English	Phonetic	Translation
Roman	/ˈrəʊmən/	
room	/ruːm/	
round	/raʊnd/	
round ▶ come round	/raʊnd/ /kʌm ˈraʊnd/	
round ▶ have friends round	/raʊnd/ /hæv ˈfrendz raʊnd/	
roundabout	/ˈraʊndəbaʊt/	
routine	/ruːˈtiːn/	
routine ▶ dance routine	/ruːˈtiːn/ /ˈdɑːns ruːˈtiːn/	
royal	/ˈrɔɪəl/	
rubber	/ˈrʌbə(r)/	
rugby	/ˈrʌgbɪ/	
rude	/ruːd/	
rules	/ruːlz/	
run off with	/rʌn ˈɒf wɪð/	
running, go running	/ˈrʌnɪŋ, gəʊ ˈrʌnɪŋ/	

S

English	Phonetic	Translation
safe	/seɪf/	
safely	/ˈseɪflɪ/	
said ◀ say	/sed, seɪ/	
sail	/seɪl/	
salad	/ˈsæləd/	
salmon	/ˈsæmən/	
salt	/sɒlt/	
same	/seɪm/	
sand	/sænd/	
sandwich	/ˈsænwɪdʒ/	
sank ◀ sink	/sæŋk, sɪŋk/	
sardine	/sɑːˈdiːn/	
sausage	/ˈsɒsɪdʒ/	
save	/seɪv/	
saw ◀ see	/sɔː, siː/	
say	/seɪ/	
scar	/skɑː(r)/	
science	/ˈsaɪəns/	
Scotland	/ˈskɒtlənd/	
Scouts	/skaʊts/	
screech	/skriːtʃ/	
sea	/siː/	
seaside	/ˈsiːsaɪd/	
see	/siː/	
see ▶ **We'll see about that!**	/siː/ /wiːl ˈsiː əbaʊt ˌðæt/	
seem	/siːm/	
send	/send/	
sent ◀ send	/sent, send/	
serious	/ˈsɪərɪəs/	
set off	/set ˈɒf/	
shape	/ʃeɪp/	
shark	/ʃɑːk/	
sharp	/ʃɑːp/	
ship	/ʃɪp/	
shoe shop	/ˈʃuː ʃɒp/	

English	Phonetic	Translation
shop	/ʃɒp/	
shopping centre	/ˈʃɒpɪŋ sentə(r)/	
short	/ʃɔːt/	
shot up ▶ my hand shot up	/ʃɒt ˈʌp/ /maɪ ˌhænd ʃɒt ˈʌp/	
should	/ʃʊd/	
shoulder	/ˈʃəʊldə(r)/	
show	/ʃəʊ/	
shower	/ˈʃaʊə(r)/	
Shrove Tuesday	/ˈʃrəʊv ˈtʃuːsdeɪ/	
shy	/ʃaɪ/	
sights	/saɪts/	
signs	/saɪnz/	
silly	/ˈsɪlɪ/	
similar	/ˈsɪmɪlə(r)/	
singer	/ˈsɪŋə(r)/	
sink	/sɪŋk/	
sit	/sɪt/	
size	/saɪz/	
skate	/skeɪt/	
skateboard	/ˈskeɪtbɔːd/	
skiing	/ˈskiːɪŋ/	
skills	/skɪlz/	
skin	/skɪn/	
sleep	/sliːp/	
slim	/slɪm/	
slow	/sləʊ/	
slowly	/ˈsləʊlɪ/	
small	/smɔːl/	
smuggler	/ˈsmʌglə(r)/	
snake	/sneɪk/	
sneakers (American English)	/ˈsniːkəz/	
snow	/snəʊ/	
snowboard	/ˈsnəʊbɔːd/	
snowing ▶ (it's snowing).	/ˈsnəʊɪŋ/ /ɪts ˈsnəʊɪŋ/	
snowman	/ˈsnəʊmæn/	
so	/səʊ/	
so ▶ I think so.	/səʊ/ /aɪ ˈθɪŋk səʊ/	
soap opera	/ˈsəʊp ɒprə/	
soccer (American English)	/ˈsɒkə(r)/	
sofa	/ˈsəʊfə/	
some	/sʌm/	
someone	/ˈsʌmwʌn/	
sometimes	/ˈsʌmtaɪmz/	
soon	/suːn/	
Sorry!	/ˈsɒrɪ/	
sort ▶ all sorts of things	/sɔːt/ /ɔːl ˈsɔːts əv θɪŋz/	
Sounds great!	/saʊndz ˈgreɪt/	
soup	/suːp/	
south	/saʊθ/	
south-east	/saʊθ ˈiːst/	
south-west	/saʊθ ˈwest/	
Spanish	/ˈspænɪʃ/	

English	Phonetic	Translation
speak	/spiːk/	
special	/ˈspeʃl/	
spend money	/spend ˈmʌnɪ/	
spend time	/spend ˈtaɪm/	
spicy	/ˈspaɪsɪ/	
spider	/ˈspaɪdə(r)/	
spiky	/ˈspaɪkɪ/	
spoke ◀ speak	/spəʊk, spiːk/	
sponsored	/ˈspɒnsəd/	
sports programme	/ˈspɔːts prəʊgræm/	
sports shop	/ˈspɔːts ʃɒp/	
sporty	/ˈspɔːtɪ/	
spring	/sprɪŋ/	
squirt	/skwɜːt/	
stand	/stænd/	
stand up	/stænd ˈʌp/	
star	/stɑː(r)/	
star wars	/stɑː wɔːz/	
start	/stɑːt/	
start time	/stɑːt taɪm/	
statue	/ˈstætʃuː/	
stay	/steɪ/	
stay ▶ have friends to stay	/steɪ/ /hæv ˈfrendz tə steɪ/	
stay over	/steɪ ˈəʊvə(r)/	
stay up	/steɪ ˈʌp/	
steam boat	/ˈstiːm bəʊt/	
step	/step/	
step ▶ dance steps	/step/ /dɑːns steps/	
stick	/stɪk/	
sticker	/ˈstɪkə(r)/	
still	/stɪl/	
stomach	/ˈstʌmək/	
stop	/stɒp/	
Stop it!	/ˈstɒp ɪt/	
storm	/stɔːm/	
story	/ˈstɔːrɪ/	
straight	/streɪt/	
Straight after lunch.	/ˌstreɪt ɑːftə ˈlʌntʃ/	
straight on	/streɪt ˈɒn/	
strange	/streɪndʒ/	
strap	/stræp/	
street	/striːt/	
strict	/strɪkt/	
strong	/strɒŋ/	
studio	/ˈstjuːdɪəʊ/	
study	/ˈstʌdɪ/	
style	/staɪl/	
stylish	/ˈstaɪlɪʃ/	
subject	/ˈsʌbdʒɪkt/	
suddenly	/ˈsʌdnlɪ/	
sugar	/ˈʃʊgə(r)/	
suitcase	/ˈsuːtkeɪs/	
summer	/ˈsʌmə(r)/	

English	Phonetic	Translation
sun	/sʌn/	
sunglasses	/ˈsʌnglɑːsɪz/	
sunny ▶ It's sunny.	/ˈsʌnɪ/ /ɪts ˈsʌnɪ/	
sunscreen	/ˈsʌnskriːn/	
supermarket	/ˈsuːpəmɑːkɪt/	
superstar	/ˈsuːpəstɑː(r)/	
supper	/ˈsʌpə(r)/	
sure	/ʃʊə(r)/	
surf	/sɜːf/	
surfboard	/ˈsɜːfbɔːd/	
surprise	/səˈpraɪz/	
sweater (*American English*)	/ˈswetə(r)/	
sweatshirt	/ˈswetʃɜːt/	
sweets	/swiːts/	
swimming	/ˈswɪmɪŋ/	
swimsuit	/ˈswɪmsuːt/	
swing	/swɪŋ/	
switch off	/swɪtʃ ˈɒf/	
T		
take	/teɪk/	
take ▶ It takes an hour.	/teɪk/ /ɪt teɪks ən ˈaʊə(r)/	
talent show	/ˈtælənt ʃəʊ/	
talk	/tɔːk/	
tall	/tɔːl/	
tall ▶ How tall are you?	/tɔːl/ /haʊ ˈtɔːl ə juː/	
tea	/tiː/	
team	/tiːm/	
teenager	/ˈtiːneɪdʒə(r)/	
teeth	/tiːθ/	
television	/ˈtelɪvɪʒn/	
temple	/ˈtempl/	
tennis	/ˈtenɪs/	
tent	/tent/	
than	/ðæn/	
Thanks.	/θæŋks/	
that	/ðæt/	
That's £1.99 please.	/ðæts ˈwʌn naɪntɪ ˌnaɪn pliːz/	
That's why ...	/ðæts waɪ.../	
theatre	/ˈθɪət ə(r)/	
theme park	/ˈθiːm pɑːk/	
then	/ðen/	
thin	/θɪn/	
thing	/θɪŋ/	
think	/θɪŋk/	
think of	/θɪŋk əv/	
thirsty, be thirsty	/ˈθɜːstɪ, bɪ ˈθɜːstɪ/	
this	/ðɪs/	
thought ◀ think	/θɔːt, θɪŋk/	
thousand	/ˈθaʊzənd/	
threw ◀ throw	/θruː, θrəʊ/	
through ▶ through the streets	/θruː/ /θruː ðə ˈstriːts/	
throw	/θrəʊ/	

English	Phonetic	Translation
thunder	/ˈθʌndə(r)/	
ticket	/ˈtɪkɪt/	
tidy	/ˈtaɪdɪ/	
tiger	/ˈtaɪgə(r)/	
tight	/taɪt/	
till	/tɪl/	
time	/taɪm/	
time ▶ have a good time	/taɪm/ /hæv ə gʊd ˈtaɪm/	
times	/taɪmz/	
tired	/ˈtaɪəd/	
tip	/tɪp/	
tobacco	/təˈbækəʊ/	
toe	/təʊ/	
together	/təˈgeðə(r)/	
tomato	/təˈmɑːtəʊ/	
tomorrow	/təˈmɒrəʊ/	
tongue	/tʌŋ/	
tonight	/təˈnaɪt/	
too	/tuː/	
took ◀ take	/tʊk, teɪk/	
tooth	/tuːθ/	
top	/tɒp/	
toss	/tɒs/	
touch	/tʌtʃ/	
tour ▶ on tour	/tʊə(r)/ /ɒn ˈtʊə(r)/	
tourist features	/ˈtʊərɪst fiːtʃəz/	
towards	/təˈwɔːdz/	
town ▶ go into town	/taʊn/ /gəʊ ɪntə ˈtaʊn/	
track	/træk/	
track ▶ karting track	/træk/ /ˈkɑːtɪŋ træk/	
trail, treasure trail	/treɪl/ /treʒə treɪl/	
train	/treɪn/	
trainers	/ˈtreɪnəz/	
travel	/ˈtrævl/	
trick	/trɪk/	
trip	/trɪp/	
trouble ▶ get into trouble	/ˈtrʌbl/ /get ɪntə ˈtrʌbl/	
true	/truː/	
try	/traɪ/	
T-shirt	/ˈtiː ʃɜːt/	
tummy	/ˈtʌmɪ/	
tuna	/ˈtʃuːnə/	
turkey	/ˈtɜːkɪ/	
turn	/tɜːn/	
turn off	/tɜːn ˈɒf/	
turning	/ˈtɜːnɪŋ/	
TV	/tiː ˈviː/	
U		
ugly	/ˈʌglɪ/	
Ugh!	/ʌg/	
UK	/juː ˈkeɪ/	
umbrella	/ʌmˈbrelə/	

English	Phonetic	Translation
uncle	/ˈʌŋkl/	
under	/ˈʌndə(r)/	
understand	/ˌʌndəˈstænd/	
uniform	/ˈjuːnɪfɔːm/	
United States	/juːˌnaɪtɪd ˈsteɪts/	
until	/ənˈtɪl/	
up	/ʌp/	
us	/ʌs/	
use	/juːz/	
usual	/ˈjuːʒʊəl/	
usually	/ˈjuːʒəlɪ/	
V		
Valentine's Day	/ˈvæləntaɪnz deɪ/	
vegetables	/ˈvedʒtəblz/	
very	/ˈverɪ/	
view	/vjuː/	
vinegar	/ˈvɪnɪgə(r)/	
visit	/ˈvɪzɪt/	
voice	/vɔɪs/	
volcano	/vɒlˈkeɪnəʊ/	
W		
wait	/weɪt/	
wake up ▶	/weɪk ˈʌp/	
She wakes me up.	/ʃɪ weɪks mi: ˈʌp/	
Wales	/weɪlz/	
walk (n.)	/wɔːk/	
walk (v.)	/wɔːk/	
wall	/wɔːl/	
wallet	/ˈwɒlɪt/	
walls	/wɔːlz/	
want	/wɒnt/	
warm ▶ It's warm.	/wɔːm/ /ɪts ˈwɔːm/	
washing-up ▶	/wɒʃɪŋ ˈʌp/	
do the washing-up	/du: ðə wɒʃɪŋ ˈʌp/	
waste	/weɪst/	
watch (n.)	/wɒtʃ/	
watch (v.)	/wɒtʃ/	
Watch out!	/wɒtʃ ˈaʊt/	
water	/ˈwɔːtə(r)/	
water pistol	/ˈwɔːtə pɪstəl/	
water sports	/ˈwɔːtə spɔːts/	
waterfall	/ˈwɔːtəfɔːl/	
wavy	/ˈweɪvɪ/	
way ▶ a long way	/weɪ/ /ə lɒŋ ˈweɪ/	
wear	/weə(r)/	
weather	/ˈweðə(r)/	
weather ▶ the weather	/ˈweðə(r)/ /ðə ˈweðə(r)/	
We'll meet in the usual place.	/wiːl ˌmiːt ɪn ðə juːʒʊəl ˈpleɪs/	
week	/wiːk/	
weekend	/ˈwiːkend/	

English	Phonetic	Translation
We got into a lot of trouble.	/wiː gɒt ɪntʊ ə lɒt əv ˈtrʌbl/	
welcome	/ˈwelkəm/	
well	/wel/	
Welsh	/welʃ/	
went ◀ go	/went, gəʊ/	
west	/west/	
wetsuit	/ˈwetsuːt/	
what?	/wɒt/	
When is … on?	/wen ɪz … ɒn/	
where?	/weə(r)/	
which?	/wɪtʃ/	
whistle	/ˈwɪsl/	
white	/waɪt/	
who?	/huː/	
whose?	/huːz/	
Why don't we …?	/waɪ dəʊnt wiː…/	
why?	/waɪ/	
wife	/waɪf/	
Will you be out for long?	/wɪl juː biː aʊt fə ˈlɒŋ/	
win	/wɪn/	
wind	/wɪnd/	
window	/ˈwɪndəʊ/	
windy ? **It's windy.**	/ˈwɪndɪ/ /ɪts ˈwɪndɪ/	
wing	/wɪŋ/	
winner	/ˈwɪnə(r)/	
winter	/ˈwɪntə(r)/	
wish	/wɪʃ/	
witch	/wɪtʃ/	
with	/wɪð/	
woman	/ˈwʊmən/	
work	/wɜːk/	
worksheet	/ˈwɜːkʃiːt/	
world	/wɜːld/	
World Cup	/wɜːld ˈkʌp/	
worry ▶ **Don't worry.**	/ˈwɒrɪ/ /dəʊnt ˈwɒrɪ/	
Would you like to …?	/wʊd juː laɪk tə…/	
wrist	/rɪst/	
wrong ▶ do something wrong	/rɒŋ/ /du: sʌmθɪŋ ˈrɒŋ/	
wrote ◀ write	/rəʊt, raɪt/	
Y		
year	/jɪə(r)/	
Yes, hold on, I'll get her for you.	/jes, həʊld ɒn, aɪl get hə fɔː juː/	
young	/jʌŋ/	
Yuck!	/jʌk/	
Z		
zoo	/zuː/	

Macmillan Education
Between Towns Road, Oxford OX4 3PP
A division of Macmillan Publishers Ltd
Companies and representatives throughout the world

ISBN 1 405 01908 5
ISBN 1 405 07405 1 (with CD Rom)

Designed by Mackerel Limited.
Illustrated by Mark Davis.
Cover design by Mackerel Limited.
Cover image by Getty.

The author would like to thank Mark Farrell for his help and support.

The publishers would like to thank the following for their kind permission to reproduce
photographs:
John Birdsall p82; Corbis pp 25(Sygma), 38(Adam Woolfitt), 71(Anne W. Krause); Empics
p18(bl); Getty pp27, 60(t), 70; Mark Farrell/ Photosforbooks pp60(b), 105(r); Rex
Interstock p105(l);

Commissioned photography by Haddon Davies pp13, 17, 26
Picture research by Pippa McNee

Printed and bound in Spain by Edelvives.
2009   2008   2007   2006   2005